PRAISE FOR

Talk IS Chief

"Talk Is Chief *is a guide to leadership at a challenging time of tweets, fake news, and growing divisions within our democracy. The simple fact is that words matter—and that simple words matter the most when they speak to our values. I often say we govern by leadership or crisis. The author makes clear that leadership requires courage in both action and communication."*

—**LEON E. PANETTA,** chairman,
The Panetta Institute for Public Policy

"Jack has brought to the forefront the critical skill necessary in managing complex organizations, navigating unimaginable crises, and leading companies to realize greatness. Communication aligns organizations, supports strong and transparent cultures, and is vital to respond to both opportunities and threats. Jack takes us through valuable lessons ranging from building effective communications structures able to capture the data necessary to make swift decisions to fostering relationships with diverse stakeholders. Intuitive, compelling, and practical for all leaders!"

—**JIM BROOKS,** chief operating officer, Control Risks

"Talk Is Chief *reminds leaders that above all responsibilities, communication must be first. Jack is spot on, declaring that great leaders not only are good personal communicators but also hire top-notch professionals who help them build and protect reputation, bring invaluable stakeholder perspectives, and give honest counsel."*

—**MELISSA BROTZ,** CMO and chief communications officer, Abbott

"Jack Modzelewski has written a must-read primer for anyone being or aspiring to become a leader and/or work in the communication industry. Read this book and learn from one of the best international communications executives."

—**GUILLAUME HERBETTE**, chief executive officer, MSLGroup, Publicis

"Communication is the foundation for effective leadership and team harmony within any organization. In his debut book, Talk Is Chief, *Jack Modzelewski takes the readers on a journey to prove the power of effective communications and gives leaders the principles needed for implementation within their own organizations. Modzelewski's forty-plus years in public relations clearly shine through the entirety of the book. His expertise, deep understanding, and thorough market research blend seamlessly together in a must-read book for management educators and business leaders."*

—**DIPAK JAIN,** president, China Europe International Business School

"There is no one more qualified to talk about the critical role of communication in driving organizational performance. Jack's experiences as journalist, corporate executive, global communications agency leader, and mentor mean he has insight to offer every leader, regardless of setting. And he practices what he preaches: you will be inspired, informed, and entertained by this book."

—**LISA MACPHERSON**, former chief marketing officer, Hallmark Cards

""Jack Modzelewski has written a must-read book for both seasoned and aspiring business leaders. In Talk Is Chief *you will learn first-hand why culture, leadership, candid communications, and a persistent focus on reinvention are the defining qualities of the world's best-run companies."*

—**DAVE SAMSON**, general manager of public affairs, Chevron Corporation

"Modzelewski's book Talk Is Chief *makes clear what many of us have known for years, which is that communication is the secret ingredient behind every great leader from Caesar to Tim Cook. It's high time leaders of all organizations understand the power of communication and use it to their advantage."*

—**PAUL A. ARGENTI**, Professor of Corporate Communication, Tuck School of Business at Dartmouth

"Talk Is Chief *will become a must-read resource for business and communications leaders committed to organizational performance. Jack Modzelewski guides readers through what results-driven communication means in today's enterprise, leveraging his experience and passion for communications coupled with research and real-life examples. As he clearly articulates, the role of the CEO today requires not only vision but the ability to reach, inspire, and influence stakeholders—from front-line employees to investors and partners—at a time of information overload. His insights are especially critical today when there is distrust of many institutions and where technology will continue disrupting how we live, work, play, and communicate."*

—**MÓNICA TALÁN**, vice president of communications, ADT

Talk IS Chief

Leadership, Communication & Credibility in a High-Stakes World

Jack Modzelewski

RosettaBooks®
New York, 2019

Talk Is Chief: Leadership, Communication & Credibility in a High-Stakes World

For information, please contact RosettaBooks at marketing@rosettabooks.com, or by mail at 125 Park Ave., 25th Floor, New York, NY 10017

First edition published 2019 by RosettaBooks

Cover design by Mimi Bark
Interior design by Christian Fuenfhausen

Illustrations courtesy of CartoonStock.com, CartoonCollections.com, Newsletter-Cartoons.com, and AbbottCartoons.com

ISBN-13 (print): 978-1-9481-2252-8
ISBN-13 (ebook): 978-0-7953-5274-4

Library of Congress Cataloging-in-Publication Data

Names: Modzelewski, Jack, author.
Title: Talk is chief : leadership, communication, and credibility in a high-stakes world / Jack Modzelewski.
Description: First edition. | New York : RosettaBooks, [2019] | Includes bibliographical references and index.
Identifiers: LCCN 2019020414 (print) | LCCN 2019980286 (ebook) | ISBN 9781948122528 (print) | ISBN 9780795352744 (ebook other)
Subjects: LCSH: Communication in management. | Communication in organizations. | Leadership.
Classification: LCC HD30.3 .M6326 2019 (print) | LCC HD30.3 (ebook) | DDC 658.4/5--dc23

www.RosettaBooks.com
Printed in the United States of America

"Speech has allowed the communication of ideas, enabling human beings to work together to build the impossible.

Mankind's greatest achievements have come about by talking. Our greatest hopes could become reality in the future. With technology at our disposal, the possibilities unbounded.

All we need to do is make sure we keep talking."

—Pink Floyd, "Talkin' Hawkin'"

(Featuring the words of Stephen Hawking)

Table OF Contents

Introduction xi

1 Leaders and Future Leaders: We Are All in Communications 1

2 Do Culture and Communication Eat Strategy for Breakfast? 17

3 "I Need a Miracle" 33

4 Anticipating Risks, Preparing for Opportunities 65

5 Sizzle in the Narrative 89

6 Leaders Need Communications Pros 115

7 Shift Happens 139

8 Stand Up for Change 167

9 Final Thoughts: Words as Weapons and Personal Communication Style. 191

Acknowledgments. 203

Bibliography 207

Index 213

About the Author. 219

"Clausewitz and Sun Tzu are great, but my best strategic plans come from Pinterest."

Introduction

The CEO of a global automaker projects compelling visions of opportunity in a future "mobility" industry, all while his company's stock price lags behind a bull market, costing him his job. An activist investor uses his media skills to paralyze the leadership of a company he believes is underperforming. A British CEO takes the helm of an iconic American company with goals to restore its "mojo." And an Asian leader becomes the undisputed political boss and "storyteller in chief" of the second-largest economy in the world.

These are among the tales and anecdotes featured in *Talk Is Chief: Leadership, Communication & Credibility in a High-Stakes World*, which drives home Sir Winston Churchill's statement that "the difference between mere management and leadership is communication." Churchill knew. Not only was he a masterful communicator, but he was also the only sovereign leader to win the Nobel Prize for literature. But make no mistake, he worked very hard at his wordsmithing and used clever and inspiring rhetoric as the lubricant of his leadership communication style.

This book is about the inseparable link between leadership and communication. It is about common problems and opportunities facing leaders and the use of strong and timely communications to address them. I am talking about situations that require leaders to rally people around a cause or mission. Getting out of messy situations or avoiding them entirely. Or influencing key stakeholders to change their perceptions about where an organization is heading versus where it's been.

Think about what leaders do. They communicate plans, goals, values, rewards, and good and bad news to people. Once they have communicated, leaders expect people to do what they have asked: Make those numbers. Go out and get the vote. Take that hill. Beat the pants off those other guys.

Leadership cannot happen without the right communication. Leaders provide the who, what, when, where, and how of their grand plans. But they must not forget the *why*. They must specify *why* people are being asked to do things to fulfill their leader's goals. Command and control organizations are as passé as the Yellow Pages.

Leadership communication cuts along the razor's edge of both reward and risk. Opportunities abound for leaders to use communication to influence urgency, energy, and inspiration. To clarify mission, direction, and purpose. To advocate cultural continuity or needed change. To ignite competitive and innovative spirit. To display authenticity, confidence, integrity, and humility. To promote collaborative partnership and diplomacy. Leadership communication does all this and more, giving leaders the intelligence, influence, and victories they seek.

A new generation of rising leaders has embraced communication—in all its social platforms and digital-age forms—like no other generation before. Yet they, too, make mistakes. Young entrepreneurs learn, sometimes the hard way, that credibility and trust must be earned every day. And that it can evaporate quickly should a leader stumble. The same applies for veteran executives. Those who climb the leadership ladder without practicing strong communication skills are like the pilot with early-morning passengers who are half-asleep: He can talk all he wants on the in-flight intercom about his route to a destination, but who is listening?

Leaders are dependent on their communication skills while performing up to 90 percent of their executive responsibilities. Are top-notch communication skills and instincts now a requisite for ascending to—or trying to keep—leadership positions? More than ever. One can argue that strong communication abilities are as important to contemporary leaders as their fiduciary, operational, talent recruitment, deal-making, and other executive skills.

A study conducted by Egon Zehnder confirmed this. The study showed that "CEOs not only allocate an unexpectedly large amount of time and attention to corporate communications (as much as half of their working day) but also acknowledge its key strategic significance: they emphasize the growing importance of communication in terms of overall corporate strategy. ...As these CEOs see it, communication has itself become part of the strategy and therefore a core business management function in its own right."

Whether viewed as a core management function or as the most important activity a leader performs, I believe leadership communication is a big factor in success or failure, for reasons spelled out in the pages ahead.

In his book *Outliers*, Malcolm Gladwell said that in addition to talent, it takes ten thousand hours to master a skill or a profession. I have been a public relations consultant, communications executive, and journalist for four decades. I figure that I have spent close to one hundred thousand hours toiling in the communications profession, while evolving and learning the new ways required to navigate in this golden age of communications and public relations.

That's why I have focused on communication as a critical factor in leadership success, and maybe the most important aspect of a leader's scope of influence. I offer that premise from observing many leaders in action, and from my own personal experience as a corporate leader with P&L, human capital, and other leadership responsibilities.

You may already be a leader. Maybe you run a public company. Or started your own firm. Or head up a national or local not-for-profit organization or a membership-based association. Or lead a government entity—a city, a state, a police department, or some other unit delivering services to the citizens. Or maybe you are studying business and want to learn communication strategies and skills to help propel you into a leadership position.

No matter your position, you must understand how to communicate in all directions: up to boards of directors and governing bodies; laterally to investors, customers, and business partners; and systemically to everyone in your organization.

I hope that in addition to the practical advice, you will enjoy some of my storytelling, which is meant to amplify instructive points. No doubt I have left out a few good stories and thus promise to post more on my website, which you can find at www.JackKnifePR.com.

"Any questions?"

1

Leaders and Future Leaders:
We Are All in Communications

> *"Communication shouldn't be just another hat that a CEO wears. It should be at the core of everything you do."*
>
> **—Scott Beck, CEO of CHG Healthcare**

Leaders need to be heard and clearly understood above the constant noise of the complicated worlds in which they must lead or govern. The stakes in this new communication environment are high.

How high?

In survey after survey, the data suggests that leadership communication—for organizations and brands—is critical to trust, reputation, and approval. But some surveys report that high-value communication is getting short shrift from organizational leaders. Many leaders still seem to underappreciate—and underperform—their vital communication responsibilities to their many stakeholders, particularly their own employees. A recent Gallup study found that only 13 percent of American employees think that the leadership of their companies communicates effectively with the rest of the organization. And only 15 percent believe that their companies' leadership inspires enthusiasm about the future.

In addition to Gallup, you can look at recent studies from the Ketchum Leadership Communication Monitor, the Golin-U.S.C. Annenberg Global Relevance Review, PwC's Global CEO Survey, and other sources. The pattern is similar.

If leaders are not motivating and driving desired behaviors, aren't they risking organizational complacency, irrelevance, and even failure? Of course.

At the same time, it has been demonstrated that leadership can add substantial value to enterprise performance, marketplace advantage, and the loyalty of customers, workers, members, and other constituencies. How so?

- **Communication provides the thematic skyway for people to visualize the pinnacle of performance.** That's why leaders must clearly tell people what they expect, congratulate them when they deliver on those expectations, and then tell them what they need to do next.

- **Strong cultures can be extremely productive** so long as their leadership continually leads them forward, in both words and actions. That means constantly communicating new threats and opportunities, while reminding everyone what made them historically successful, if not dominant, in the past.

- **Leadership communication is the oxygen that breathes purpose, passion, and personalized meaning into the organization.** It provides the "why us?" narrative, explaining why the organization exists and what makes its products, services, and standards superior to the rest.

- **Leaders also may be in a better position to head off existential risks** before they occur, through better vertical and lateral communication within their organizations. That is something we'll examine in more detail later.

But with leadership communication must come results. Active leadership communication alone will not Teflon-coat a leader in every situation. Let's look at two leaders who took the helm in succession at one of America's oldest companies—Ford Motor Company.

After Henry Ford's great-grandson Bill Ford decided he could not fix the problems that he took upon himself as Ford's CEO from 2001 to 2006, his board of directors brought in Boeing executive Alan Mulally to take over as chief executive.

Mulally was credited with a remarkable turnaround at Ford, even though it apparently was not sustainable after his tenure ended in 2014. But few turnaround CEOs faced Mullaly's early challenges, most notably a financial crisis: the company suffered a record $17 billion loss in 2006, the year he joined as CEO.

He also faced a cultural challenge with an executive team that, as Mulally described, was uncomfortable sharing problems and bad news in meetings with their leader and executive-team peers.

Mulally changed that reticence his first year at the helm of Ford. He encouraged executives to collaborate and cooperate more to fix systemic problems impeding marketplace success.

"In 2006, Mulally donned his Superman cape and led one of the greatest comebacks in American business history," wrote columnist Joe Nocera of *Bloomberg News*. "As Ford's chief executive, he not only made Ford hugely profitable. He also revived employee morale, turned a backstabbing culture into a collaborative one and replaced secrecy with openness. Oh, and the stock? It generated annualized returns of 10.4 percent during his eight-and-a-half-year tenure."

In mid-2014, as he left the automaker, Mulally told *Bloomberg News* that whatever he achieved at Ford was also relevant to other organizations: "I am more convinced than ever, after doing this for 45 years, in the power of a compelling vision, a comprehensive strategy, and a management system where you manage that [strategy] relentlessly."

He went on to say that when everyone is on board with both the vision and the plan to execute it, "all of us contribute to that … and we all want to help each other. And I think that works in profit, nonprofit, or any organizations that are trying to deliver something very important."

Mulally may have been echoing the words of U.S. President Ronald Reagan, who said, "The greatest leader is not necessarily the one who does the greatest things. He is the one that gets people to do the greatest things. Leaders lead others to do big things."

Mulally was a tough act to follow for his successor, Mark Fields, a Ford career veteran. Fields is an example of failure based on the disconnect between leadership vision and financial performance. During his CEO tenure, many saw him as charismatic, transformative, media savvy, and visionary. But his communication abilities, with which he was gifted, could not overcome disappointing performance by Ford. Under pressure from shareholders and his board of directors, he resigned less than three years after becoming CEO.

Days after Fields's "voluntary" ouster, legendary auto industry executive Bob Lutz took a different view of Fields's fall from grace. He labeled Fields "an old-fashioned, typical automotive CEO." That was interesting coming from Lutz, who was in his mid-eighties and thirty years older than Fields.

Lutz, a former fighter pilot, has never been characterized as typical. When I did some work for Chrysler earlier in my career, Lutz was known for "testing" hot Chrysler cars such as the Viper at high speeds on the streets in and around Detroit.

"There was no excitement coming out of the company," Lutz said of Fields's tenure, speaking on CNBC's *Squawk Alley*. "Nowadays if you don't sell the sizzle, you are not going to be able to market the steak." Lutz went on to make sharp comparisons. One was a contrast of Fields's balanced, steady, conservative style of not projecting too far into the future with Elon Musk's more hyperbolic vision of an automotive industry adapting to his own disruptive and innovative forces at Tesla.

Lutz also contrasted the two companies' stock prices at the time, with Tesla achieving nosebleed market-cap valuations and the exuberant investor support normally accorded red-hot technology companies. (Elon Musk would later prove that through misguided communication and tweeting he could make Tesla's stock price dramatically descend the same way it soared.) Ford's stock had declined to bargain-basement status, losing 36 percent of its value during Fields's tenure as CEO.

The argument Lutz made was that a CEO should not be judged only by "day-to-day performance"—and Ford's performances were by some measures pretty good under Fields—but also by the ability to communicate better things to come, to excite car buyers and the people who lend to and invest their capital in big enterprises.

The *Wall Street Journal* took a different view, decidedly more short-term versus visionary. It commented that Fields lost momentum by placing too much exploratory attention on future "smart mobility" services and new technologies for a "post-car" era of transportation. The *Journal* observed that Fields should have continued Mulally's "one team" game plan and figured out how to sell more Ford cars and trucks in more places.

A Very Public Occupation

A leader's strengths and style as a communicator can be a difference maker. Fields probably thought he was hitting the right notes with his communication. But when boards and shareholders become restless, leaders get the heave-ho.

You can substitute a lot of leaders in place of Fields in scenarios where impatience trumps transformative vision. There is so much emphasis on short-term performance that visionaries trying to change the game must get beyond promises and projections and prove that it's working.

Leaders who wish to be taken seriously need to take seriously what they say and the communications advice they receive.

The actions of leaders are always under scrutiny. Their words are often assailed by doubting investors, activist critics, rumor traffickers, and media chatterists.

And there are plenty of situations in which misinterpreted words or nuances can draw leaders into turbulent situations—including disagreements with their employees, directors, and shareowners, or with politicians, unions, and special interest groups. "Leadership is a very personal and very public occupation," said Terry Pearce, a business author and global leadership trainer, in a video for the firm BlessingWhite.

Perhaps there was a time when leaders, with the exception of political leaders, could hide their communication inadequacies, if not their indifference to or contempt for public attention. They could intentionally shun a high profile. Or as movie mogul Lew Wasserman suggested, "Stay out of the spotlight. It fades your suit."

Jack Welch was not one of them.

Communication Is a Two-Way Street

Welch, the chief executive of General Electric for two decades, knew the importance of communication for leaders. "In leadership you have to exaggerate every statement you make," Welch told the authors of the book *Lessons from the Top*. "You have to repeat it a thousand times. Overstatements are needed to move large organizations."

Welch, like Winston Churchill, overcame an early-life speech impediment and devoted serious attention to leadership communication opportunities and performances. Those who worked closely with Welch knew that he understood that communication is a two-way street, and that leaders must also be patient listeners and comprehend the critical practice of *being understood.*

Whenever leaders put words into action and actions into words, they put their personal reputations and those of their organizations on the line.

In that regard, Jeff Bezos, the founder and leader of Amazon, put it well: "A brand for a company is like a reputation for a person. You earn reputation by trying to do hard things well." Yet there was a time when investors were skeptical of the "hard things" Bezos and Amazon were trying to do—until Amazon did them. With amazing outcomes. It is well-known that Bezos, a *Star Trek* fan, has a space exploration company called Blue Origin. Perhaps he was inspired by Gene Roddenberry's "To boldly go where no man has gone before." To say that Amazon today is disrupting many industries may be an understatement. Meanwhile, Bezos has experienced scrutiny and criticism of his personal brand.

Leadership communication can be a key driver of reputation and brand—providing reasons why people choose to work for, buy from, or advocate for an organization. High-performance organizations are not possible without the inspiring leadership communication that tests the limits of human creativity, ingenuity, and perseverance, compelling people to give their collective best, to be "all in." That includes organizations of every kind: small businesses, governments, universities, public service, research institutions, unions, religious organizations, NGOs, civic organizations, associations, societies, and not-for-profits.

In an age when many leaders have achieved true celebrity status like Bezos, we have come to expect some leaders to be superheroes—even though, of course, they are mere mortals. Which brings to mind Ralph Waldo Emerson's observation: "A hero is no braver than the ordinary man, but he's braver five minutes longer."

Leaders must act consistently to build and then protect the reputations of the entities they lead, in good times and bad. They must focus every day on communicating a sense of trust with multiple communities of stakeholders who work for, buy from and support, and invest in their organizations.

Communication Is Chief

While I was president of European operations for a global public relations agency, I wrote an article in *CEO Today*, a British publication, on "The Power of Communication." In it I said, "Because we place CEOs on iconic pedestals, we also expect them to be dynamic communicators. A CEO has to take on the role of communication leader."

I also said the leader "can elevate the importance of corporate reputation by treating it as the measurable asset that it is, even if accounting practices may treat it as an intangible asset."

Scott Beck, CEO of CHG Healthcare, agreed with that viewpoint in an article he wrote for *Entrepreneur* magazine. "When I was named CEO two years ago, I thought I knew what I wa
for," he said. "I quickly realized, however, that th
wrong. Rather than chief executive officer
job was really to be chief communic

I like Beck's attitude, but there
leadership communication from the

communications officer. In the modern organization, leadership and leadership communication are shared responsibilities.

In organizations that are highly team oriented, there can be many important players engaged in the daily need to communicate mission-driven messages to different audiences. In that sense, they are leadership-communication partners. There may be one chief executive, but every organization needs lots of leadership from many leaders working collaboratively toward the same goals. The insecure chief who tells others, "There is only going to be one leader around here," does so at the risk of demotivating potential leaders and their contributions to performance.

Sheikh Mohammed bin Rashid Al Maktoum, vice president and prime minister of the United Arab Emirates and ruler of Dubai, knows that leadership and leadership communication are best when shared. "Life has taught me that some enterprises rely on a single leader, others rely on a team. But a one-man show enterprise is temporary," he wrote in a LinkedIn post. "Great organizations invest the most in the well-being of their people, as great leaders nurture and invest in the leaders yet to come. A leader's legacy endures when he empowers his people."

Large organizations need both the CEO and chief communications officer in separate positions, working together in common purpose. Leaders have enough to worry about. They are pulled and pushed daily in so many directions. Everyone wants more meetings, more interaction, more face time with them. They must thus rely on highly professional communication chiefs raise the level of the leader's personal effectiveness in communicating to multiple stakeholders inside and outside their ations, and across continents. Which is why I devote a pter later to leaders and their communications officers.

Better Informed, Busier. But Better Communicators?

Many twenty-first-century leaders have had to become globalists in their vast networks of "community" relationships. In an article in *Chief Executive* magazine, Jeffrey Sonnenfeld, senior associate dean of the Yale School of Management, offered this: "Once known as pillars of their local communities, now CEOs charged with massive global companies created by M&A rollups are rarely as active in local civic associations—nor do they hold the same heroic aura. The CEOs of today are better informed, busier, and more accountable than their predecessors of 40 years ago. They also endure far more grueling travel schedules, cope with more demanding constituencies on shorter time frames, face tougher scrutiny, and feel more lonely than their predecessors."

Sonnenfeld's observation is true about the demands on business leaders. But his article—entitled "Back to the Future: How 40 Years Has Changed the CEO Post"—does not mention that communication has become central in the life of today's leaders.

Unfortunately, most business schools don't emphasize strategic leadership communication in their curricula. Business schools do a disservice to future leaders by not recognizing that leadership success is highly dependent on the strong personal communication skills of leaders. Dartmouth's Tuck School of Business is not one of them.

Paul Argenti is a professor of corporate communications and corporate responsibility at Tuck. He is also a business consultant and someone I have had the privilege to work with in the past. Argenti is one professor-counselor who believes leaders need to be vibrant communicators. "The ability for a leader to move people through communications cannot be underestimated," Argenti said in a talk entitled "The CEO's Speech." "I don't think there's anything more important."

Gradually, Then Suddenly

But sustaining a good reputation for a company and its leadership is not easy. Even worse, reputation can be a here-to-day-gone-tomorrow phenomenon. In Ernest Hemingway's *The Sun Also Rises*, a character named Mike Campbell was asked how he went bankrupt. His answer: "Two ways. Gradually and then suddenly."

That is also how leaders and their organizations can lose credibility, customers, investors, their reputations, and much more. Gradually and then suddenly.

It can creep up on reputable leaders perceived as doing a good job, until suddenly perceptions change and confidence in their leadership declines. This happened at Ford, Chipotle, Target, Avon, Caterpillar, Tyson Foods, General Electric, and many other companies.

And it certainly happens to leaders caught up in corporate scandals or personal impropriety. Consider the former CEOs of Wynn Resorts, Intel, Wells Fargo, Volkswagen, CBS, Equifax, the Weinstein Company, Uber, Anbang, Priceline, Petrobras, Takeda, Tokyo Electric Power, Fox News Network, FIFA, Crown Resorts, Olympus, Barclays LLC, Backpage, Kobe Steel, and many more. In 2018, the *Wall Street Journal* reported that according to Liberum Research, more than nine hundred CEOs "resigned, retired or were fired in 2017 at publicly traded North American companies, the most in a decade."

It also happens to heads of state, political leaders, and university presidents. We could go on and on through different institutional categories and count up the fallen leaders.

Gradually, then suddenly works in positive ways, too.

There are leaders who gradually earn credibility and public trust. Over time they become celebrated for earning good organizational and personal reputations. Some become icons and heroes. In this category we find Michael Bloomberg, Narendra Modi, Paul Polman, Anand Mahindra, Christine Lagarde, Jamie Dimon, Bono, Frederick Smith, Paul Volcker, Wang Jianlin, Meg Whitman, Howard Schultz, Warren Buffett, Oprah Winfrey, Bernard Tyson, Leon Panetta, Sheryl Sandberg, David Rubenstein, and many others.

We Are All in Communications

As I started writing this book, I was asked to talk to a class of undergraduate students at the Stern School of Business at New York University one warm winter day. The class was composed largely of finance and accounting majors. Before beginning my remarks, I posed a few questions to the group: "How many of you want to work in big corporations or financial institutions?" More than half raised their hands. "How many of you want to become entrepreneurs or work for start-ups?" Several raised their hands. But when I asked, "How many want to work in communications?" only one woman raised her hand.

I then came to the critical point. "You all will be in communications," I said to many quizzical looks. "Because no matter what type of organization you work for, communication will be a big part of your job. Especially if you aspire to hold management or leadership positions. It will be as important as anything you study here at NYU."

That statement was an eye-opener for the class, but not for the professor, Howard Geltzer, who thanked me later for saying it. After all, like me, he had spent much of his long career in public relations and communications.

He knew exactly what I meant. Now you do, too. We're all in communications. And leadership and communication are inseparably linked.

Key Insights and Observations

- Leadership communication today is a strategic management function. Twenty-first-century leaders must embrace communication as an agenda enabler and as an empowerment platform for others.
- The stakes in this new communication environment are high.
- Communication takes 50 to 90 percent of a modern leader's day, whether s/he recognizes it or not.
- Whenever leaders put words into action and actions into words, they put their personal reputations and those of their organizations on the line. We live in an age when people expect their leaders to communicate clearly and transparently with them.
- Leadership is a shared responsibility.

"Anyone besides Ulrich have anything negative to say about my leadership?"

2

Do Culture and Communication Eat Strategy for Breakfast?

"Leadership is hard to define and good leadership even harder. But if you can get people to follow you to the ends of the earth, you are a great leader."

—Indra Nooyi, former CEO of PepsiCo

In successful cultures, leaders communicate with both well-chosen words and with timely actions. Some call it walking the talk.

I always believed as an executive I would never ask my subordinates to do what I was not willing to do myself. Ours was a culture where executives were producers and doers. I guess that is known as leading from the front.

In the fall of 2013, when states supporting the introduction of Affordable Care Act health insurance plans were mounting their marketing efforts to enroll the uninsured, my agency FleishmanHillard was part of a multi-agency team focused on enrolling people in the Get Covered Illinois program. The campaign was massive, and the message was complicated and misunderstood. Obamacare at the national level was assailed with problems, both technical and political.

The team working on the campaign was getting lost in the details and logistics, due in part to a particular client contractor who made every day miserable with carping, nitpicking, and poor leadership. On the eve of the official October 1 start date for enrollment, I gathered our team in a large conference room and conveyed passionately the real goal of our work.

Our mission was not just to enroll people in a controversial plan mandated by the government. Whether or not we agreed in full with the intentions of the ACA, it was our job to empathize with the uninsured people whose lives we were trying to make better—especially those among the millions of uninsured with medical conditions and who needed health insurance coverage immediately.

So I asked my colleagues to think about the uninsured and put themselves in their shoes when telling the story. Our team took this as a rallying cry to transcend anything that had frustrated them about the campaign up to that point. They knew they needed to get busy making it serve those who needed to enroll. In the weeks that followed, we worked side by side on the program as I made the success of the campaign a personal and a team priority.

In the end we exceeded everyone's expectations and enrolled hundreds of thousands of people. And we did equally well in the second year of the program. Being a product of a can-do culture, I knew that we could transcend all the obstacles frustrating a team determined to push hard to the finish line. Going the distance—for better or worse—must be in a leader's DNA, or maybe he has to be a little bit compulsive. Alibaba's founder Jack Ma has been called "Crazy Jack" for his far-reaching ambitions for Alibaba and his commensurate stamina. "A leader should have higher grit and tenacity and be able to endure what the employees can't," Ma once said. Revered by his employees, Ma has also been addressed as "Teacher Ma."

Corporate or institutional culture represents collective behavior, beliefs, work ethic, ethos, mission, and legacy. It is what Terry Pearce, executive coach and former Charles Schwab senior vice president of executive communications, called "one of the central responsibilities of leadership." He went on to say, "It's to build an environment where authentic communication ... is valued and can take place."

Culture plays a big role in how a leader communicates inside and outside an organization. Does culture really eat strategy for breakfast in the business world, as Peter Drucker, the renowned management consultant, famously stated? Clearly, without a strong culture, business strategy alone may not drive performance and sustainable success. Drucker also said, "Communications is less about information as it is about facilitating a kinship within the culture. If the culture is a meritocracy and a place where humility starts at the top and where respect for the individual worker is second nature to all, then the leader will likely communicate in that fashion. He or she will avoid self-promotion and hyperbole and be modest in taking credit for the firm's performance and success. More likely that most communication from the leader will use the word *we* and not *I*, and will emphasize the merits of shared purpose, teamwork, and collaboration."

Driving Culture

John Chambers played a major role in shaping the culture of enterprise technology giant Cisco during his twenty-year tenure as chief executive officer. "Companies have very strong and great cultures," said Chambers, now chairman emeritus of Cisco. "A huge part of a leadership role is to drive the culture of the company and to reinforce it."

Leaders who communicate in collaborative, team-oriented ways must demonstrate their words with consistency of behavior. They cannot turn a blind eye to incompetence or to cutthroat and corrosive practices. It is up to leaders in the end to make the cultural values authentic and not platitudes on conference room walls.

"Every business that makes money will tell you how great their culture is, and every business that loses money will say how bad their culture is," said Kenneth Griffin, CEO of Citadel, in remarks to a meeting of the Chicago Club. In other words, you can't blame failure on culture alone, nor overly credit culture for success.

Griffin acknowledged that people generally are conflict averse. "They tolerate underperformance by people down the hall and are uncomfortable to confront them," he said. "They tolerate incompetence in others, not realizing that one person's mistake or incompetence could be catastrophic for the whole company. CEOs may not be able to prevent every mistake, but they can set the tone for oversight." He noted that in a true meritocracy, it's about "who can do the hard stuff. So you test people, perhaps beyond what you think their limits are. You take a risk on people you believe will rise to the occasion. A meritocracy is about dealing with what really matters."

Lou Gerstner, the former CEO of IBM and, earlier, Nabisco, had some pretty direct advice about corporate culture in a 2016 commentary published in the *Wall Street Journal*. He said that "companies' cultures are largely defined by what they tell their employees are the highest priorities, not what's listed in their values or purpose statements. Those priorities can be: making and growing profits, satisfying customers better, etc. Reward systems and compensation determine behavior."

Gerstner acknowledged that "creating expectations and communicating goals is a worthy and important responsibility of corporate leaders." In essence, people respond more directly to urgent needs communicated by their supervisors—not by goals stated in an annual report. All true. Most corporate employees don't even read their own annual reports. For that matter, most shareholders don't read them, either.

Perhaps that is why Allstate, in its 2018 annual Prosperity Report (the company's relabeling of its annual shareholders report), democratized leadership. "Everyone is a leader at Allstate," said the company's human resources chief, Harriet Harty. "We have six leadership principles that guide and empower employees. These principles define our culture, drive our business results, and are embedded in talent recruitment and performance management."

Operate Globally, Act Locally

Organizations that span multiple continents know that the transference of knowledge, values, and proven cross-border business practices are key to commercial success. While cultures and customs differ from place to place, including regions like the EU and North America, how does an enterprise focus on a common commercial culture? In fact, many companies do it well. Some NGOs and governments do, too. For instance, Japanese companies that have traded in foreign countries like the U.S. for the past half century have foundational principles and yet are still attuned to the cultural differences and sensitivities of employees, communities, and customers. Some have referred to this as *glocalization*. Operate globally, act locally.

Leaders must appreciate that mid- to large-sized organizations have microcultures. The culture in one function or department, or one country versus another, may be quite different than what exists at headquarters—even if everyone believes in the same organizational mission and goals.

Laurence Fink, who heads up BlackRock, the largest asset-management firm in the world, believes that "talking about culture every day" is the reason his company is one of the most successful firms of its kind. He told an Economic Club of Chicago audience that corporate culture at his global firm is not "some BS conversation that's etched on a wall; it's how we live every day." He said it's a matter of connecting BlackRock employees across one hundred countries and continually emphasizing the firm's long-term purpose of serving its investment customers while staying "connected with society to build a better future for our clients" in all of its communities.

"There is not a day in my job, there is not a business trip where I don't focus on [BlackRock's] culture," Fink said. "And all the leaders do that. We obviously try to live that culture we talk about." He added that also means maintaining a multilocal orientation by "being a Japanese firm in Japan" and "being a Mexican firm in Mexico."

Harry M. Jansen Kraemer Jr., the former chairman and CEO of Baxter International, is now a professor at the Kellogg School of Management at Northwestern University. I met him several times when working on Baxter engagements. In his book *From Values to Action: The Four Principles of Values-Based Leadership,* Kraemer emphasizes the need to relate better to Baxter employees in Japan, Mexico, and other countries, including those working in manufacturing plants.

"When you are a global company," Kraemer wrote, "the ability to relate to others takes on another dimension, crossing borders and cultures as you interact with people whose language and customs are different than yours. Our ability to understand how and why they do things will enhance your ability to relate to them."

Despite globalization, some companies commit cultural offenses. Marriott International, a highly reputable hospitality company, clearly offended the government of the People's Republic of China when it listed Taiwan, Tibet, and Hong Kong as separate countries in an online and mobile survey sent to guests and rewards-program members. Marriott acknowledged the mistake and apologized, but not before China's Cyberspace Administration launched an investigation and demanded that the U.S. hotelier suspend its Chinese website.

On a more serious scale, Volkswagen faced the reality of its German-centric culture in the wake of a massive international scandal, which impacted its European and U.S. markets. The company was investigated for falsifying test results for carbon dioxide engine emissions, specifically by installing in millions of its cars software designed to underreport emissions. After allegations first hit in 2015, the situation became progressively worse, resulting in eight million cars recalled in Europe and half a million in the U.S. Ultimately, sales declined. The global CEO was ousted and later indicted in the U.S. The company has paid more than $25 billion in fines, penalties, and lawsuit settlements. Ultimately, sales declined and VW's market value declined precipitously. Needless to say, all of this sullied the German automaker's reputation.

Hinrich Woebcken, the CEO for Volkswagen's North American region, joined the embattled German carmaker in early 2016, one of the lowest points for the company. "In my thirty years of business experience, I never had such a challenge as to manage a crisis and at the same time build a future," Woebcken said at a 2018 auto show in the U.S. He cited "brutal honesty" and "getting [my] team behind me" as key factors in getting VW back on track.

In the midst of managing the crisis, Woebcken recognized an opportunity to challenge his company's Eurocentric culture and suggested a new business model for Volkswagen in North America. Rather than taking all marching orders from VW's German headquarters, Woebcken convinced his boss and the board of directors to allow the North American branch of the company to be more independent in order to expedite decisions and plans more quickly. "Maybe the crisis helped," Woebcken concluded. "Maybe the shock told the company to let the American guys do what they need to do."

Crisis can lead to new leadership that often challenges brand and cultural status quo. After a few significant *E. coli* scares that tarnished a formerly strong brand image, Chipotle appointed a new leader from competitor Taco Bell. Despite the past food-related crises, Chipotle CEO Brian Niccol pointed to a larger issue in his mind. "I believe the brand has been invisible. This brand needs to be leading culture, not reacting to it," Niccol said shortly after taking the top job at Chipotle.

Fast Growth Foments Stress

A 2015 cover story in the *Economist* on "Reinventing the Company" compared the old cultural models of publicly listed companies to the twenty-first-century entrepreneurial model that has spawned incredible innovations and high-performance private companies. The article noted that start-ups were "pioneering a new organizational form. The central difference lies in ownership: whereas nobody is sure who owns public companies, start-ups go to great lengths to define who owns what. Early in a company's life, the founders and first recruits own a majority stake—and they incentivize people with ownership stakes or performance-related rewards. ...This aligns interests and creates a culture of hard work and camaraderie."

But certain companies that grow explosively in the absence of an identifiable culture generate tensions and problems. For example, as allegations of sexual harassment swept through Uber, its board grappled with what to do. Eventually, CEO and Uber founder Travis Kalanick resigned, followed by other senior executives. Kalanick sent a company-wide email, saying that "if we are going to work on Uber 2.0, I also need to work on Travis 2.0 to become the leader that this company needs and that you deserve." But his board preempted that personal transformation.

Working to contain the Uber controversy was writer and entrepreneur Arianna Huffington, at that time the lone woman on the board. She recognized that the company's operational style under Kalanick's leadership had generated great internal stress and burnout among employees. An advocate of work-life balance and observer of challenges women face in male-dominated organizations, Huffington was a key player in the board's decision to replace Kalanick.

Fast-growing companies encounter cultural tensions at some point or another, with common issues of how people are treated and what kinds of behavior are tolerated. Company culture begins with leadership. Note the use of "2.0" in Kalanick's statement. It's common parlance in technology product evolution, as every improvement seems to deserve a new number. But it also reminds me of what F. Scott Fitzgerald once said, "there are no second acts in American lives."

While many believe Fitzgerald meant that personal redemption (and its modern technology industry equivalent, 2.0) isn't possible, others suggest another angle: that Americans who fail want to skip Act Two entirely and go straight to Act Three, whereby their misfortunes recede and they rebuild reputations lost.

An editorial in the *Wall Street Journal* attempted to put the former Uber leader's downfall in perspective: "The only story the business press likes better than a glorious start-up is an inglorious failure, so Mr. Kalanick is now getting a rough ride. But he's built an innovative business that fulfills a public need, and Uber's investors had better hope his replacement is as good a manager as Mr. Kalanick has been an entrepreneur." The search for Kalanick's replacement ultimately led to Dara Khosrowshahi, former CEO of Expedia.

Other fast-growing tech companies have grown into global giants and yet seem to have managed cultural growth more successfully. Jeff Bezos and his team have built Amazon from an online bookseller into an e-commerce giant, diversifying into cloud computing, grocery retailing, drones, space travel, and other businesses. It has now become a career destination for business school grads.

Cultural considerations and communication are really important activities during a C-suite transition. A McKinsey & Company survey entitled "Ascending to the C-Suite" found that the nearly twelve hundred executives surveyed ranked "the creation of shared vision as the most important transition activity." Once the new vision is shared, "mobilizing teams to function as a high-performing group" was next in importance.

The McKinsey study noted that "executives reporting the most successful transitions stand out from the rest in how they built buy-in and communicated a vision to their teams and their organizations." Executives leading successful transitions were also more likely to communicate which corporate programs or initiatives should cease, given new priorities for the organization. A principle of good leadership communication is to clarify new directions, spelling out what people should de-emphasize or discontinue, whether it is halting production on poor-selling products or curtailing travel.

One such challenge is when a CEO takes the helm after a merger and must combine two distinct cultures. Historically, companies have had mixed success in merging two different cultures, especially when strategic priorities and value systems are mismatched.

Communications As a Weapon

Given the perennial trend of consolidation in so many industries and professions, cultural misalignment remains a big challenge. Leaders are golden if they can mastermind mergers and acquisitions while also minimizing the disruption of, and fallout from, cultural mash-ups. Leadership communication, in fact, is one of their best weapons.

In *Chief Executive* magazine, Elise Eberwein, chief communications officer at American Airlines, described the experience working under her boss, CEO Doug Parker, after U.S. Airways bought and merged with American in 2013.

"For those on the legacy U.S. Airways team, there was much familiarity with Doug's leadership style and vision," Eberwein wrote. "But Doug was adapting to a larger and more complex business and that group needed to adapt as well. For those on the legacy American side, there was certainly more hesitancy around speaking openly without having had that history with their new CEO."

Eberwein noted that Parker used his Monday leadership meetings to bring the two airline cultures closer together. "Doug Parker is a very approachable leader, and his direction at those Monday morning gatherings relayed something even more critical; that is, what kind of culture the new company was going to aspire to create. Here, allowing one's vulnerabilities to show through and using humor were two of the behavior attributes that helped create a unified team of leaders very quickly after our merger."

Chief communications executives can be major facilitators between leadership and the rest of the organization. "Today's CCOs must be able to operate in areas where they had previously only played a supporting role," former General Electric CCO Gary Sheffer wrote in a *Fortune* article. "Take 'culture' (everything an enterprise does and how it does it). Because culture is essential to a strong reputation ... CCOs now partner with HR to understand the passions and aspirations of their colleagues, and to express this collective purpose simply and persuasively."

Leadership communication is an ongoing process that stimulates change in organizations, shapes new cultures and refreshes the status quo, and helps translate vision into progress and prosperity.

And it really matters in a crisis.

Key Insights and Observations

- Communications can be a powerful force to establish united purpose and kinship throughout an organization.
- Organization culture, shaped and sustained by leaders, is a key driver of why people choose to work for, buy from, or advocate an organization. Culture plays a big role in how a leader communicates inside and outside an organization.

- Culture is one of the central responsibilities of leadership: to build an environment where authentic communication is valued and can take place.
- Culture reflects what an organization prioritizes and preaches. But it can also be what a company turns a blind eye to, which can range from incompetence to cutthroat, corrupt, or corrosive practices.

"Crisis? Which crisis?"

3

"I Need a Miracle"

> *"Bad companies are destroyed by crisis. Good companies survive them. Great companies are improved by them."*
>
> **—Andrew Grove, former CEO of Intel**

A prominent CEO of a global company and his assistant are on their way to the World Economic Forum (WEF) in Davos, Switzerland, where the CEO will participate in panel discussions and hold private meetings with heads of state and corporate leaders. After the CEO's private Gulfstream V lands in Zurich, a Mercedes SUV waiting on the tarmac transports him and the aide to a private area of the airport, where a helicopter is waiting to whisk them to the snow-covered resort village of Davos. Once the helicopter is airborne, however, it quickly veers off course. Instead of flying east, toward Davos, the pilot heads west and then sharply south.

By the time the CEO realizes that the pilot and copilot are speaking a language he does not recognize, the copilot has a pistol to his head and is telling him to remain calm. The CEO realizes that he and his assistant have just been kidnapped by a terrorist organization. Within an hour they will land at a private helipad, where the two hostages will be bound and blindfolded, and then transferred to an unmarked van and taken to an unknown destination. Those waiting to greet them at the Stilli helipad in Davos become concerned when the helicopter does not arrive after its scheduled thirty-five-minute flight time.

When the terrorist organization behind the kidnapping contacts the World Economic Forum leadership, it demands that the forum suspend its agenda for the week and that the leaders of six major countries immediately release members of the terrorist organization currently jailed in their prisons.

This could be the opening to a thriller written by David Ignatius or Dan Brown. But while it features a fictional scenario, the threat it represents is anything but inconceivable.

Crises Define Organizations and Their Leaders

Lucky is the leader who never faces a career-testing crisis. But most leaders will at one time or another have to clear their agendas to deal with a major incident or highly combustible problem—one that lasts days, weeks, or even months. Still, not every serious problem needs to turn into a crisis. How a leader deals with an escalating problem can prevent a crisis from fully erupting, or at least mitigate its impact before it metastasizes. Slow or inadequate action is likely to exacerbate a problem. And poorly timed or ill-conceived communication will only make matters worse.

But before the leader can communicate, he or she must comprehend the size and gravity of the problem, all while the drama is unfolding. This scenario requires Mr. Decisive, not Mr. Dithers.

Every Crisis Has Fingerprints

Crisis is an overused word. I like the *Merriam-Webster* dictionary's definition of a medical crisis: "The turning point for better or worse in an acute disease or fever." A crisis is when events build to a critical moment whereupon outcomes are greatly affected by decisions—or the absence of them.

Any largely unsolved societal problem today is called a crisis. In the U.S. we have the opioid drug crisis. Mass shootings and the urban violence crisis. The immigration visa crisis. The college campus assault and rape crisis.

Around the world, we have sovereign debt crises. In Syria, Myanmar, and other countries torn by civil war and unrest, we have humanitarian, refugee, and human rights crises. Human trafficking is a worldwide crisis. Famine is a crisis. As if we don't already have enough real crises in our world, filmmakers invent new ones. Movies about zombie apocalypses, global disease pandemics, alien invasions, and world-ending calamities. Young film viewers seem to enjoy dystopian plots, especially ones in which superheroes save mankind from archvillains.

I define crisis as something where a threat is almost existential, and severe mishandling can send an organization into paralysis or freefall. At the same time, few big companies in crisis ever close their doors; they generally re-emerge after bankruptcy proceedings, are acquired by another organization, or are nationalized. (Note that I use the words *severe mishandling.*) That said, company names and brands do occasionally disappear in the wake of a crisis. Think Enron, Arthur Andersen, Barings Bank, Long-Term Capital Management, and Sears and many other retailers.

I have witnessed many heated debates in boardrooms and situation rooms when dealing with red-hot crises. When a crisis occurs, one of the first questions asked is whether the leadership team anticipated the crisis or was caught off guard. Either way, if a company is prepared, it can respond immediately with action. Communication may be directed to the public only in part; leaders and their problem-solving teams often do their best strategizing, fact gathering, directing, and communicating behind closed doors.

The "Right" Thing to Do

Crises bring out the best in some leaders. Some possess an extraordinary ability to process incomplete information and make critical judgments while arriving at what they think is the best thing to do. Maybe even the "right thing" to do. Blessed are the organizations with such leadership—the ones who face adversity with courage, urgency, and the steadfastness to see the situation through to its conclusion.

Mary Barra, for example, was the newly appointed CEO of General Motors in January 2014 when she became an overnight business icon. She had been celebrated in the media for not only being the first woman to lead a global automaker, but also for rising through the ranks of the company over three decades after getting her hands dirty on assembly lines prior to becoming a GM executive, and for leading major corporate functions such as product design and engineering.

Barra's CEO "honeymoon" period lasted only weeks. Her leadership was severely tested during an ignition-switch failure on certain older models of Chevy cars. The problem was massive, dating back more than a decade. Plaintiffs' lawsuits filed in multiple states alleged that the ignition-switch defect caused accidents resulting in hundreds of deaths and casualties. GM would ultimately recall twenty-nine million vehicles and pay compensation to more than a hundred victims and their families. In addition, Barra faced months of negative headlines and the ordeal of testifying in back-to-back hearings before congressional committees.

Back in Detroit, Barra made crucial decisions during the first weeks of the crisis. She appointed a former U.S. prosecutor to conduct an investigation as to why the ignition-switch defects had not been reported years earlier to the C-suite and the board of the company; fired fifteen executives and appointed a new head of product safety; pushed new internal policies designed to encourage employees to promptly bring any safety issues to the attention of management; and brought in outside attorney Kenneth Feinberg to handle the task of reviewing all ignition-switch claims against the company. A skilled dispute mediator, Feinberg had served as the U.S. government's special master of the September 11th Victim Compensation Fund and later as the government's special master for TARP (Troubled Asset Relief Fund Program) executive compensation.

Barra also demonstrated skill and courage in her leadership communications. She spoke with reporters, gave updates at town hall meetings, and met with the families of accident victims. In short, she never ducked for cover. "I never want to put this behind us," she told employees at one point. "I want to put this painful experience permanently in our collective memories."

Those unfortunate leaders who falter during a rapidly escalating crisis may find their organizations or brands in the headlines for what seems like an eternity—or at least until someone else's bad luck or behavior knocks them from the front pages. Many endure being ridiculed on late-night entertainment TV shows or becoming clickbait on pseudo-news websites.

The goal, of course, is to avoid becoming late-night fodder and clickbait in the first place.

In business, mistakes are made in product design and planning, manufacturing, and customer relations. But they often can be overcome quietly. Big communication mistakes are difficult to keep quiet or overcome quickly.

Take the case of Dr. David Dao, who was dragged off an overbooked United Express aircraft in 2017 by Chicago Department of Aviation police after refusing to accept a monetary voucher and a seat on a later flight. Four passengers were chosen randomly by computer to surrender their seats on UA flight 3411. Three did. Dao, a sixty-nine-year old immigrant from Vietnam, refused to exit the aircraft. Video captured and posted online by horrified passengers showed Dao, who suffered injuries, screaming as he was dragged down the aisle and off the plane by airport police.

Overbooking is a common practice among airlines. But was it necessary to drag a screaming passenger off the plane? Of course not. CNN headlined a story "United mired in epic PR disaster," a sentiment echoed by the *Wall Street Journal* in an editorial: "As corporate PR fiascoes go, the United Airlines case of the doctor forcibly dragged off an overbooked flight at Chicago's O'Hare International Airport Sunday is one for the ages."

In retrospect, the incident did not have to become an "epic

PR disaster." That came as a result of United's underwhelming and misguided response in the first twenty-four to forty-eight hours, especially on the part of its CEO, Oscar Munoz. In fact, Munoz's response is what turned the episode into a bigger, more embarrassing story.

Munoz's initial public statement was viewed as defensive and tone-deaf: "This is an upsetting event to all of us here at United. I apologize for having to re-accommodate these customers. Our team is moving with a sense of urgency to work with authorities and conduct our own review of what happened. We are also reaching out to this passenger to talk directly with him and further address and resolve this situation."

The statement was lampooned on late-night talk shows, with Jimmy Kimmel calling it "sanitized, say-nothing, take-no-responsibility, BS speak." The brickbats on social media poured in and piled on the CEO as rarely before seen, many using the Twitter hashtag #UnitedBadPR. Many were vicious, including one that read, "United CEO Munoz turns lemons into cyanide."

I was compelled to tweet a comment of my own: "UA CEO should give the mistreated customer free airfare for life, only after creating common-sense training at UA." Of course, after posting my comment, I realized that Dao would likely sue United for all that his lawyers could win in a settlement, and that he probably would never fly United again. But the theme of using common sense echoed through all the news coverage and social media commentary about United's crisis management.

It was not until a few days after the incident that Munoz gave his first television interview, to Rebecca Jarvis, a reporter for ABC News. His initial answers to her questions showed an apologetic CEO who admitted that his company had been "shamed" by what happened on Flight 3411.

Jarvis then asked the question we all wanted to ask: What went wrong? Munoz, striking a conciliatory pose on camera, gave a measured reply: "It was a system failure. We have not provided our front-line supervisors and managers and individuals with the proper tools, policies, procedures that allow them to use their common sense. And this issue could have been solved by that. That's on me. I have to fix that." He went on to say that United would immediately begin reviewing many of its policies, including access by law enforcement personnel to its aircraft. He promised it would "never happen again."

But why hadn't Munoz and his executive team already put those types of policies and procedures in place, given that Munoz had publicly gone on record as saying he wanted to see United provide a better overall customer experience?

Munoz would survive the crisis, but for a period of time his personal reputation circled the drain. United would later pay an undisclosed settlement, which personal injury litigators estimated to be eight figures.

The United fiasco demonstrates why it is so important to be prepared for almost anything and to respond correctly from the get-go. It's amazing that a global transportation company that had been through fatal plane crashes, hijackings, employee strikes, and bankruptcy could fumble a manageable situation. But it did.

Go Big or Go Home

Working to contain crises is something I have done since the 1980s. In fact, before my baptism by fire working on a crisis from the PR side, I was a news reporter during the 1982 Tylenol crisis. That's when seven people died after taking Extra-Strength Tylenol capsules that had been laced with cyanide by an unidentified perpetrator and placed on store shelves throughout the Chicago area. In a textbook example of best practices in crisis management, Johnson & Johnson, the maker of Tylenol, quickly moved to recall thirty million units of Tylenol products (not just capsules) nationally, a move that cost the company millions of dollars but resulted in widespread commendation for its CEO, James Burke. Tylenol sales rebounded in the year following the tragedy, as did the company's stock price.

Johnson & Johnson handled the Tylenol crisis in a way that was rooted deeply in the company's values and credo. Why didn't Johnson & Johnson anticipate the possibility of tampering and design a technology to prevent it? Maybe because what occurred at the time was unthinkable. But the tragedy did result in a long-term consumer safety benefit: tamper-resistant packaging and product design changes that have become standard across the pharmaceutical world.

The financial markets meltdown of 2008–2009 took several CEOs and leaders down. But others survived, and in some cases, their firms came back even stronger. Ken Griffin, CEO of Citadel, was one of those CEOs. At a Q&A session with a Chicago business club audience, he talked about his global investment firm's plunge during the financial crisis of 2008–2009.

"We lost $13 billion in assets in sixteen weeks," Griffin told the group. "But we were determined *not to go down.* Most hedge funds would have folded after that. We communicated clearly and directly to our investors, creditors, and shareholders our plan that we were going to survive. We communicated our plan to come back. As we were dealing with this, we had news trucks parked outside our building waiting for us to announce bankruptcy."

In the fall of 2008, there was talk on the street that Citadel, like Lehman Brothers, was illiquid and seeking a government bailout to avoid going under. But Griffin knew the rumors were simply the product of panic, and that Citadel's financial position was not as dire as perceived to be. On advice from one of his key investors, he went public with that story, opening his books to investors and, as a result, convincing them not to exit his hedge funds.

He also kept his team together and informed and continued to treat his employees well. Even though the firm was and still is known as a tough and highly competitive workplace, résumés poured in from macroeconomic traders and quantitative analysts who wanted to work there. Citadel roared back from the brink, with Griffin becoming wealthier and more influential in the process. Later that year, he told *Fortune* that he had built the firm to survive market crashes and other events that provoked panic selling, but that he had never expected a scenario quite like the one that shook the financial world in 2008.

In my time involved in crisis counseling, I have worked with many CEOs, corporate communication executives, general counsels, and other C-suite executives. Happily, most of them survived their crises and continued to lead their organizations for many years.

Throughout my career, I have dealt with more than twenty-five crises, including the following:

- Deadly accidents, including airline crashes, train wrecks, natural-gas pipeline explosions, and industrial catastrophes
- Listeriosis, salmonella, and other foodborne outbreaks
- Product quality and product liability issues
- Medical equipment malfunctions and failures
- Boycotts
- Class action lawsuits
- Activist-led assaults on companies and their boards, including corporate campaigns
- Executive malfeasance
- Whistleblowers
- Employee misconduct and ethical impropriety
- Sexual harassment

That seems like the gamut, but it's not the full spectrum.

Categories of Crises

What else is a crisis?

It could be a wildfire in California, an oil spill off the African coast, a dam bursting and flooding a valley in Brazil. It could be a massive electricity failure affecting millions of people, a natural-gas main explosion in a major city, a water supply shortage in a drought-stricken country, a long-shuttered nuclear energy plant leaking radioactive toxins into the environment. It could be massive financial fraud or a Ponzi scheme, a banking and financial system crisis, a product whose batteries catch fire or explode, or bacteria-tainted foods. It could be all of the above—and all happening in one year, or even less, around the world.

Today, scientists, academic experts, and authors predict crises of terrifying proportions: cyberbreaches capable of taking down entire electrical grids; superbugs and other lethal pathogens causing pandemics; shocks to the world's economies that lead to market crashes. But we also live in an age in which meteorologists can track hurricanes and other natural disasters long before they hit human populations and destroy property. Scientists can even identify the paths of meteors advancing toward Earth's orbit. And, of course, as outlined earlier, a terrorist incident in Davos at the World Economic Forum, which I have attended five times, is always a possibility. (In fact, it is likely that WEF and Swiss military and law enforcement authorities have gamed out a variety of nightmare scenarios.) All of which means few vulnerabilities should go unanticipated, no matter how low the odds of actual occurrence.

It's often been said that no one could have predicted a "black swan" like the September 11 terrorist attacks on the United States. But former members of the U.S. intelligence community have gone on the record in saying that they predicted exactly such an event in the 1990s. Apparently, mistrust and lack of cooperation among law enforcement and intelligence agencies resulted in unheeded warnings.

Similarly, according to former U.S. Federal Reserve Chairman Alan Greenspan, the Great Recession, which stemmed from the housing bubble and a subprime mortgage calamity that exploded into a near-global financial meltdown in 2008, could not have been predicted.

Yet as chronicled by Michael Lewis in his book *The Big Short*, Michael Burry of Scion Capital not only predicted it would happen, he placed huge, high-risk trades based on that prediction—investments that later paid out enormously.

Crisis situations can be grouped into categories. The first is a crisis in which a company or an organization is the victim of circumstances clearly beyond its control. Examples are massive storms and other natural disasters that result in deaths. Natural disasters, in fact, account for many of the crises reported each year. Yet natural catastrophes always seem to raise the issue of human inadequacy in foreseeing the worst, as well as how well (or poorly) governments and their response operations performed during the crisis. Hurricane Katrina will always stand out as a crisis management debacle, one during which too many human operations went wrong, exacerbating an already terrible event.

A second category of crisis involves accidents or events over which a company has some control. In China, government officials have been fired after the construction of major dams created geological stress points, spurring earthquakes. And during the Firestone and Ford tire crisis, in which the reputations of both companies were damaged as a result of Firestone tires shredding and blowing out on Ford Explorers and light trucks, more than six million tires were recalled. Lawyers representing hundreds of accident victims, as well as the families of the forty-six people who died, sued both companies.

Inevitable finger-pointing ensued, and the leadership teams of both companies were severely tested. Firestone tires were faulted, but the question remained as to why neither Firestone nor Ford recognized the potential problem earlier. This is often the case when supply chain partners are the source of a crisis, which can leave the company that sells the end product holding the bag for much of the reputational damage and litigation.

PR Can't Solve Non-PR Problems

I once had a client who was a major automotive service franchiser, and on one occasion I was sent to Philadelphia to provide PR counsel to a franchisee who was under criminal investigation for overbilling customers. My client wanted to make sure the franchisee didn't make the situation worse by pleading his case publicly.

Upon meeting the franchisee and explaining why I'd been sent, he grabbed my suit jacket lapels. "Jack, I don't need coaching!" he all but shouted. "I don't need your counsel. I need a miracle!"

I had no PR miracle tucked away in my back pocket that would keep him from being indicted. No magic wand to make it go away. In fact, I would have a very lucrative practice if I were in the miracle business. While many believe that crisis PR is like a magic act, where you redirect the audience's attention someplace else, I can tell you that hardly ever works. You may be able to broaden the problem to expose vulnerabilities across a spectrum of other similar organizations, but that does not necessarily take a company out of the crosshairs.

The franchisee's plea for divine intervention was not an isolated case. I have worked with business leaders who had trouble acknowledging that their firms had more than a "PR problem"—that they in fact had a business problem.

PR cannot solve non-PR problems. Communications and damage control will not make a serious, deeply rooted business problem go away. And that often requires calling time-out from normal business practices until the situation is remediated and the product is fixed, which can be painful and expensive but is often the only way to restore public confidence and trust. There are no shortcuts to reputation restoration, just a lot of hard work and determination to get it right.

Unfortunately, by the time problems surface for leaders, they've already become crises. Former President Barack Obama told an audience that he frequently had to deal with five crises in the same day when he was in the Oval Office. By the time something hit his desk, he said, it had morphed into a full-blown crisis mostly because no one else in his administration had known what to do about it.

Leaders just never know what awaits them when they get up in the morning. Such was the case with the Swedish retailer Hennes & Mauritz, which was forced to confront international outrage stemming from its online ad depicting a black child wearing a green hoodie emblazoned with the words "Coolest Monkey in the Jungle." Widely perceived as racist, the ad was criticized on social media by NBA star LeBron James, the rapper Sean "Diddy"

Combs, and other celebrities. In response, H&M appointed a global diversity leader, ostensibly to repair the damage and make sure its marketing people never repeated the offense. I've no doubt there were more than a few moments when H&M's leadership thought, "What the hell were they [we] thinking?"

From Cheers to Jeers

Most people experience crises in their personal lives—the unexpected death of a loved one, job loss, bankruptcy, terminal cancer, and a host of other things that bring life to a halting new reality. Sometimes personal problems spill into business issues and affect an organization's reputation and its continuity. Just consider the effect the multiplicity of sexual harassment claims against Harvey Weinstein had on him and his entertainment production company. A total reputational and financial disaster.

Or think about the CEO who was fired by his board and prosecuted by a court after surveillance video showing him abusing a friend's dog in an elevator went viral. He was supposed to be caring for the puppy, but the camera caught him repeatedly kicking the animal and yanking its chain.

Still, it can be painful to watch a public person fall from grace and glory. I have been a communication coach and trainer to many people including entertainers, professional athletes, politicians, and other public figures. In these sessions the participants are told never to lie in an interview, a press conference, or, for that matter, in any situation.

I remember training a group of corporate-sponsored professional cyclists for future media interviews. One of them was a young Lance Armstrong, long before his international success in the Tour de France and other racing events. For that and other reasons, it was especially hard to watch his life and career unravel when he finally admitted in a 2013 interview with Oprah Winfrey that, despite years of denial, he had used performance-enhancing drugs.

I wrote this about the former hero in an article for *PRWeek*: "He admitted not only to lying but also to being a 'bully,' a 'win at all costs' competitor, and an abuser of his power and influence. But he denied he 'cheated' in winning races. Maybe he now feels better to get this enormous burden off his conscience; confession is good for the soul. And his accusers must feel vindicated, though hardly satisfied. But what about his die-hard fans, his Livestrong Foundation supporters, and those wanting to give him the benefit of the doubt? They probably feel betrayed, angry, and disillusioned, but this day was coming sooner or later."

Armstrong told Oprah at one point in the interview, "I will spend the rest of my life trying to earn back trust." Trust betrayed is hard to win back. Not only was Armstrong a world-class athlete, he was also the leader of the Livestrong Foundation, a not-for-profit organization with its own followers. After his doping admissions, the foundation separated from Armstrong, though it continues its cancer awareness work and research today. Like those steep mountains he had to pedal up in the French Alps on his way to fame, Armstrong continues to face a long, tough climb to regain his reputation and prominence.

No matter the crisis, leaders must move immediately to mitigate the threat and protect people, property, and reputation. Immediate and sincere public apologies are expected. That is usually step one. Then it comes down to determining the scope of the problem, trying to figure out how bad it can get, and mobilizing teams to work collaboratively on fixing it. Disaster recovery comes later.

In such situations, leaders must communicate more than just regret and remorse to all their stakeholders. They also need to tell them what will be done, and by whom, to address the situation and make sure it does not happen again.

And even when the clock is ticking and the public attention unrelenting, leaders must mobilize any and all outside resources needed to accomplish what they promised they would do to protect the public and rectify what went wrong. Decisions need to be made, and while second-guessing of those decisions is to be expected, all actions must play out. With both news and rumors traveling at speeds that seem to defy the laws of physics, there is little time to react. Which is why crisis planning as part of overall risk management is so important (and the subject of the next chapter).

The 3-R Apology

It is common practice to advise companies to apologize as quickly as possible in the wake of a public crisis for which they are responsible. Some companies do so with a megaphone, taking out full-page ads in major newspapers to offer mea culpas and announce actions they are taking to fix problems and prevent reoccurrences. This is commonly known as the 3-R apology: remorse, resolution, and restitution.

Wells Fargo is an example of how a company's reputation fell fast and hard during revelations of a scandal, even when events leading to the crisis were long in the making. In April 2017, the company published full-page newspaper ads featuring a letter from Timothy J. Sloan.

Sloan had been appointed CEO the previous October, following Wells Fargo's payout of $185 million in government fines and its settlement of class action lawsuits to end internal and governmental investigations into the company's fraudulent retail sales practices. Sloan's ad letter promised that Wells Fargo would change the way it handled product sales–based compensation for retail bankers and that it would create an Office of Ethics, Oversight, and Integrity.

Despite becoming a poster child for attacks by critics ranging from U.S. senators to consumer advocates, Warren Buffet, one of Wells Fargo's most famous shareholders, defended it. Sort of. "I see no reason why Wells Fargo as a company, from both an investor standpoint and a moral standpoint...is in any way inferior to the other big banks with which it competes."

Another option is to issue a statement, as Uber CEO Dara Khosrowshahi did shortly after he succeeded the embattled founder, Travis Kalanick. One business publication found the apology satisfying. "People aren't going to believe instinctively that Uber actually means it," *Inc.* wrote. "Maybe it doesn't. But that's the key to a great apology—a straightforward expression of regret that actually uses the words, 'I'm sorry' (Khosrowshahi's 'I apologize' is close enough), promises to do better—and is set forth in a credible way."

Cybersecurity attacks have become a regular part of news coverage. Equifax suffered a widespread system hack resulting in 148 million customers—nearly half the population of the U.S.—having their personal identities and other vital records exposed.

The CEO and other executives were forced to resign after reports indicated Equifax knew in advance about the company's cybersecurity vulnerability.

Not only was the company slow to address it, but it then raised questions of whether the company put profits ahead of public trust. The interim CEO of Equifax, Paulino do Rego Barros Jr., opted to broadcast his apology on the opinion page of the *Wall Street Journal.* He did not mince words: "We were hacked. That's the simple fact. But we compounded the problem with insufficient support for consumers. Our website did not function as it should have, and our call center couldn't manage the volume of calls we received. Answers to key consumer questions were too often delayed, incomplete or both. We know it's our job to earn back your trust." He went on to describe how Equifax would deal with the short-term problems resulting from its inadequate public response, as well as the longer-term challenge of restoring consumer and public confidence in its services.

He also tried to do something that is fairly common in crisis management: broaden the issue to encompass either a common, unsolved industry problem, or a societal one. To that end, Barros wrote that Equifax's remedial actions and initiatives moving forward "won't solve the larger problem. We have to see this breach as a turning point—not just for Equifax, but for everyone interested in protecting personal data. Consumers need the power to control access to personal data."

While Barros's commentary was commendable, the Atlanta-based company continued to be pilloried by consumers, consumer advocates, and influencers on social media. Months after the breach, congressional leaders continued to criticize the company for not being transparent enough about the scale of the system failure.

Could Equifax have anticipated a doomsday scenario, one that was compounded by the overwhelming response inadequacies Barros outlined in his op-ed? Probably.

Negative News and Nappies

In May of 2000 I was asked to assist Procter & Gamble with a problem it faced in Germany. Greenpeace members there had publicized a study alleging that the elastic in Pampers disposable diapers (known in Europe as nappies) contained the element tributyl tin, which can impair children's developing immune and hormonal systems. Greenpeace organized one of its trademark spectacular stunts, mobilizing mothers throughout Germany to gather and burn disposable diapers outside government buildings. The resulting media attention highlighted Greenpeace's call for a worldwide ban on disposable diapers.

At this point, however, the industry was accustomed to attacks on disposable diapers, especially from proponents of old-fashioned, washable cotton diapers. While previous third-party studies had alleged links between disposable diapers and a number of diseases—everything from asthma to male infertility—P&G's position was that its rigorous testing methodology had revealed no traces whatsoever of any harmful ingredients in its Pampers products.

I had experience with P&G and knew it to be a company that takes the health of any and all of its customers, especially infants, very seriously. My first post-college job was at a New York advertising agency that did a considerable amount of work for multiple Procter brands. As a result, I understood that it operated with integrity, had high standards, and was methodically driven to be the best.

We at the epicenter of the problem had many conference calls with P&G executives. The meetings always included participation by P&G executives calling in from the Cincinnati headquarters, as well as from Brussels and Geneva.

Past experience had shown Greenpeace to be adept at big publicity stunts and relentless public pressure when going after a target. Nonetheless, a few of the German P&G executives held a vastly different view of Greenpeace than did the rest of us, and they expressed their belief that meeting with Greenpeace might actually accomplish something. After initially rejecting Greenpeace's allegations, P&G eventually examined two key factors that led the senior leadership to consider whether the company should more carefully assess Greenpeace's claims.

First, after learning that the rubber for the elastic in Pampers came from Malaysia, P&G realized it was indeed possible that tributyl tin could be present in tiny amounts. Second, the company concluded that the testing methodology commissioned by Greenpeace might well be superior to its own.

In the end, P&G turned to another source for rubber for its diapers. When other disposable diaper producers followed suit, Greenpeace claimed victory and moved on to other causes. P&G came out ahead as well: it maintained both its reputation and market share. Leadership in this case boiled down to being open-minded and accepting the idea that an activist group might well have a legitimate concern that should be taken seriously.

P&G acted responsibly in letting its scientists work out the problem and find a solution that was ultimately in the best interests of consumers—all while vigorously defending its brand via public communications. It was a resolution that P&G employees could feel good about.

Dos and Don'ts

Two stories from early in my career illustrate how—and how not—to respond in the first days following a crisis. Both cases featured a company at the center of intense public health and safety concerns. Both entailed a foodborne illness, fatalities, and multistate product recalls. But that's where the similarities end.

In the first instance, a respected longtime CEO of a food-service business could not bring himself to accept full responsibility and do what was right after his company was associated with an outbreak of listeria connected to one of its operations. Prior to the outbreak, which quickly moved from a local news story to one that garnered national headlines, the company had been associated with strong management, quality products, and good performance for its shareholders. Its chief executive was not only a model for CEO longevity but was also known as the driving force behind the company's civic, cultural, and philanthropic activities. In many ways, the CEO was the epitome of a business leader–statesman.

One day, one of the company's food-processing divisions was linked to people getting very ill, possibly from a bad batch of products. Early medical diagnoses pointed to the listeria bacteria as the cause. While there was no fully conclusive evidence yet, as the number of reported cases of illness—some severe—multiplied over the course of a few days, the story was elevated from local to national news headlines.

As I had a consulting relationship with the company, I was called back from a vacation—not for the first time—to join the team working the problem. Before my arrival, I received the client's permission to invite another counselor, Dick Starmann, to join the team. Starmann was a former client who had worked for McDonald's for twenty-seven years. Throughout his career he had experienced multiple corporate crises—everything from negative rumors about his company's supply chain to a salmonella outbreak to a mass shooting.

Once on the job, his first question was whether the company had an experienced epidemiologist on staff or retainer. It did not. That was a problem, because the Centers for Disease Control was on the case and efficiently using new information technology to connect the dots among the reported cases. Starmann quickly added a nationally known epidemiologist to the team. Today, I can't imagine any regional, national, or international food-service enterprise not having an epidemiologist on board. You need an expert to identify the potential viral patterns of a bacteria-caused illness, one who can speak the scientific language of the CDC and other public health authorities.

A few days into the situation, it became clear the CEO was unwilling to acknowledge that his company might be at fault. He was also unwilling to order a major product recall without hard evidence linking his company to the listeria outbreak. Instead, he suggested there could be other contributing environmental factors. In short, he was in denial, even as the company was fast approaching a tipping point. Decisive action was required. Not in days, but hours.

At one point, the CEO became frustrated with those of us advising a product recall. But after weighing the risks of more fatalities, increased public criticism, and eventual litigation, I and the rest of the crisis team felt we had no choice. (You may recall that in the Tylenol tampering case, CEO Jim Burke followed the same playbook, opting for a total product recall rather than risking future fatalities and the loss of his company's reputation.)

In the end, the CEO left the decision to his number two executive, the chief operating officer—in essence making him the de facto crisis team leader. After a few final questions and clarifications, the COO set the recall in motion. It turned out to be the right decision, even though weeks of damage control followed as we investigated every step of the manufacturing process to solve the mystery of how the pathogens had contaminated the product prior to packaging. We also made a significant grant to enable university research teams to study future ways to prevent a similar outbreak.

Ultimately, the company's actions to stem the crisis earned the praise of a well-respected PR commentator as one of the best-managed episodes of that year. Little did the commentator know what went on behind closed doors and how close the company had come to suffering a permanent black eye.

Though it would have tested the mettle of any chief executive and his or her team, the second incident illustrates a better way to handle a public health crisis. In the spring of 1985, between 168,000 and 197,000 people throughout northern Illinois and adjoining states were sickened by salmonella, with seven deaths attributed to the bacteria. It was then the biggest outbreak of salmonella ever reported in the U.S.

The common denominator was a specific brand of milk that was processed and sold only at Jewel Food Stores, a Midwestern grocery chain with more than two hundred stores in four states. Although salmonella is normally killed in the pasteurization process, experts surmised that pasteurized milk had come into contact with raw milk somewhere in the processing plant.

Jewel was in full emergency mode when the firm I worked for put me on the crisis team. I was only a year into my public relations career, but I had already demonstrated good business communication skills thanks to my journalism and advertising experience.

We immediately made James Henson, the president of Jewel Food Stores, available for television and newspaper interviews, and I accompanied him on many of those interviews. We also aired television commercials in which Henson appeared on camera to reassure customers that Jewel was cooperating with the health authorities to solve the problem. Meanwhile, he said, the company was using a different supplier for its milk and dairy products. In both the media interviews and commercials, Henson projected confidence and a certain Midwestern authenticity that led people to trust that Jewel was indeed on top of the situation.

The company acted swiftly to pull the products in question from their store shelves. But even when every action on a leader's part is dedicated to the public interest, things can still go awry. Jewel store employees who disposed of recalled milk by pouring it into municipal storm sewers outside their stores were captured on camera by TV crews.

The company apologized, but the Illinois attorney general sued Jewel for violating water pollution laws. Lawyers working on behalf of victims brought their own lawsuits as well. Jewel sales reportedly dipped by as much as 15 percent in the first months following the outbreak. But those sales eventually rebounded, and Henson was given more executive responsibility by the parent company a few years later.

Ten Commandments of Crisis Management

It may run counter to the inner nature of certain leaders, but in a crisis, the objective is not to win. The goal is to survive, to fight another day, to show humility and empathy throughout, and to plan for recovery and an eventual comeback. Here, then, are my Ten Commandments of Crisis Management:

1. The truth always surfaces. The best offense is to be first to get to the truth about the situation, even in the face of pushback from attorneys worried about future litigation.

2. Own the crisis and demonstrate progress and necessary change.

3. You can never gain friends, allies, and advocates during a crisis. Only before.

4. Control the communications agenda as much as possible, even if you can't control the sequence and pace of events. Communication around most crises

is driven by news media, competitors, opportunistic public officials, and adversarial NGOs and critics.

5. Never make predictions or raise false expectations about anything out of your control.

6. Speed matters. Communicate with customers and employees ASAP. They need to receive the organization's context and messaging first, before hearing it from external sources.

7. Reputation is a corporate asset, but it must be earned every day. A lost reputation *can* be regained.

8. Employees may be in the best position to spot trends—both good and bad—that affect the business. Review and intensify risk-management plans and processes to prevent aftershocks or a crisis continuum (more on this in Chapter 4).

9. Avoid finger-pointing and circular firing squads in your own organization. A caveat: if you are the leader of a government or political entity, point away. Identifying the source of the problem may be unavoidable, since the media, including citizen journalists, always requires a villain.

10. A cover-up can kill a company, and you, as the leader, with it.

In addition, here are tips and general principles that will both help prepare you for a crisis and mitigate it while it is happening:

- Communication in a crisis must be integrated and multichannel and dovetail with the organization's mission. It must also agree with an organization's narrative, community relationships, and legal considerations.

- Equip a workspace as a designated "war room" in advance of a crisis.

- A frequently updated (I suggest quarterly) and approved organizational narrative defining who you are, what you do, etc., should be at the ready.

- Breaking news forces organizations to respond to new developments. To keep up, an expedited legal approval process for all outbound statements is crucial.

- Global organizations need tested systems in place to communicate with executives and staff in all the countries and time zones in which they operate. This includes phone numbers for texting and instant messaging.

- Local executives need to be prepared to respond to their local employees, customers, business influencers, and other key stakeholders. Give them what they need and refresh as necessary.

- Social media experts must monitor perceptions and commentary around the clock. It's the best way to track and anticipate what external forces may be in

> play and can intensify a crisis. This data may also point to what the organization needs to do to best satisfy or mute critics. Look to political campaigns, which have become skilled in this realm.

The truth is, not every crisis is an explosion, a terrorist attack, an airplane crash, or a financial market computer systems flash crash. Sophisticated technology allows ship captains to see icebergs, both real and proverbial, well enough in advance to correct course. Similarly, organizations have the technology and experts at their disposal to enable them to watch for signs of danger on the horizon.

Good leaders know that bad events can be severely disruptive, bringing an organization to the point of paralysis. They confront difficulties head-on and try to convert emerging serious issues into positive pivots.

That is why risk management, the subject of the next chapter, is so vitally important.

Key Insights and Observations

- Crises define organizations and their leaders.
- Not every serious problem needs to turn into a crisis, which makes this chapter a good prelude to risk-management practices.
- No matter the crisis, leaders must move immediately to mitigate the threat and protect people, property, and reputation.
- PR cannot solve non-PR problems. The best communications and damage control will not make a serious, deeply rooted business problem go away.

RISK
MANAGEMENT

4

Anticipating Risks, Preparing for Opportunities

"I always say that my job is not to think about today. My job is to look around the corner and feel and see what's coming, and then warn everybody else."

—Angela Ahrendts, former Apple executive and former CEO of Burberry

You may ask why are there so many crises that appear to have been preventable. It's a good question and one analyzed next.

Unlike crisis management, which is largely reactive, risk management, with its goal of crisis anticipation and preparation, is a proactive process.

Great organizations and companies do not become great without their leaders taking risks. Some risk every penny, piastre, or peso they have, plus everything they can borrow, for the chance to become the next Amazon, Alibaba, or Airbnb.

Leaders of nations, companies, and other organizations take risks, calculated and sometimes miscalculated, while making watershed decisions and straddling dilemmas. Even with guidance from trusted advisers, leaders frequently make these decisions alone. They must then live with the consequences.

Walt Disney saw risk this way: "Courage is the main quality of leadership, in my opinion, no matter where it is exercised. Usually it implies some risk—especially in new undertakings." Disney combined ambitious dreams, risks, and courage to create one of the world's greatest entertainment empires.

This chapter, however, is not about telling entrepreneurs how to take risks. Instead, it offers advice on foreseeing and managing risks once an organization is established. Risk-taking can lead to great success, but risk ignorance can result in costly failure.

It makes no difference if an organization is one hundred years or one hundred weeks old. Whether you are a start-up with twenty people or a Fortune 500 organization, you face both short-term and longer-term risks. If you have created something worth sustaining, why would you allow it to decline or even die due to poor risk management?

Most management teams pay close attention to immediate risks and take steps to retain dissatisfied customers and top-performing employees. They can respond rapidly to marketplace moves by a feared competitor. Such threats are fairly common. But it's the longer-term risks and threats, the ones buried under layers in larger, more complex organizations, that can surface like crocodiles in a lake.

I believe not enough time and attention is devoted to risk management in organizations. Leaders and employees spend most of their time making good products and keeping customers, investors, and other stakeholders happy. Why ruin this by neglecting worst-case-scenario planning?

Companies, governments, and other organizations face a variety of risks that can become potential calamities and disruptions, such as:

- Natural disasters
- Industrial accidents
- Cybercrime
- Sabotage and security breaches
- Intellectual property and data theft
- Fraud
- Espionage
- Government investigation
- Major government policy changes
- Boycotts
- Prolonged employee strikes
- Activist shareholder actions
- Unfair or corrupt trade practices
- Negative social media campaigns and innuendo
- Disruptive game-changing competition
- Litigation

Prevent the Preventable

Most bad things that happen to companies and organizations are preventable. Sometimes they are a result of something as simple as old-fashioned human error in the age of quick-triggered computer programs, attributable to a few people rather than institutional process. Mistakes like the false missile alarm that shocked the people of Hawaii—and visiting professional golfers and tourists—one quiet Sunday morning in 2018. The emergency alert was rescinded after thirty-eight minutes, but not before considerable psychological damage and chaos had ensued. "For nearly 40 minutes, it seemed like the world was about to end in Hawaii, an island paradise already jittery over the threat of nuclear-tipped missiles from North Korea," the Associated Press reported.

Larger problems left unattended are likely to become full-blown crises. It could be a single employee allegation of sexual harassment that later turns out to have been a pattern (Fox News Network). It could be product failure resulting in a massive recall (Samsung). It could be an industrial accident, with fatalities and environmental damage (BP). It could come from sourcing product ingredients from another country, where quality inspections are systemically lax and labor practices abusive (Lumber Liquidators).

It often takes years, sometimes decades, to build a good reputation—a reputation that can be tarnished or destroyed in just days. And it may not be a single deed or misdeed that is responsible for the damage.

With all the demands on a leader's time and priorities, he or she would generally prefer to put energy where it will be best recognized—creating jobs, generating economic value, making good things happen. Preventing risks from becoming crises isn't rewarded enough by boards of directors, shareholders, voters, and others who ultimately judge a leader's performance.

Henry M. Paulson Jr., the former U.S. Treasury Secretary and Goldman Sachs leader, knows this all too well. Reflecting on his stressful years at Treasury from 2006 to 2009, he told an audience at the Stanford Graduate School of Business, "You don't get credit for preventing a disaster people don't see."

Paulson recalled telling President George W. Bush and his economic team at a 2007 Camp David meeting that something major—some big financial crisis—was looming. Bush asked him what might cause it. Paulson replied that he couldn't be specific but conjectured that the crisis could stem from derivatives and credit default swaps, or perhaps from subprime loans. A year later he was proved right.

Several years later, I sat next to Paulson at a private dinner and heard a firsthand account of the most difficult days in his brief government career, a story about how government officials and financial experts had not sufficiently anticipated and prepared better for the collapse of Lehman Brothers and the government-led bailout of Bear Stearns, Fannie Mae, Freddie Mac, AIG, the largest banks, General Motors, and Chrysler. (Paulson first addressed these issues in his 2010 book, *On the Brink*, and in his many public appearances in the decade since the crisis.) In retrospect, Paulson and others received credit for stemming a black swan type of crisis and preventing a global collapse of the financial markets.

Leaders cannot emphasize risk identification enough. They must periodically take time from driving the business to huddle with their leadership teams and share worst-case scenarios. Once potential risks are vetted, the communications team and other functional leaders should conduct exercises to build readiness and test reaction speed. It's my experience that companies with real situation plans often fail in their reaction time because they don't perform drills on a regular basis. Public safety organizations routinely run drills, and all other organizations should follow suit. Today, crisis-scenario simulations can be conducted globally and virtually through private platforms connecting the key players who will be called upon in a real situation.

But if you are truly trying to build a culture in which risks are considered openly so that you can get ahead of the curve, start with these fifteen questions:

- Have you disrupted your own organization? Conduct opposition research on your own company and stage a mock attack, just as politicians do when preparing for a campaign.

- Do you have a system in place for monitoring threats and issues that can turn into nightmare scenarios?

- Is the crisis-situation team ready to deal with the scenarios you anticipate? Does the team meet periodically to discuss the threats?

- Beyond a general crisis plan, do you have a playbook for different crisis scenarios?

- Do your stakeholders trust you and you them? If not, get these relationships in a better place before it's too late! Once a crisis is underway, you'll need them. Which third-party supporters will stand by you in a crisis and not duck for cover?

- Have you pressure-tested the crisis team as well as the plan?

- If a crisis does occur, what other major issues or problems will likely be disclosed, leaked, or investigated? What might reignite a firestorm once you think you are in the clear?

- Are there potential problems you can anticipate and prevent now, before they get worse?

- Have you audited your internal culture to detect any credibility gaps that disconnect the company's stated values from how it actually behaves?

- How ready are your internal communication systems to reach employees across all locations?

- Do you have a business-continuity task force in place?

- Have you conducted multistakeholder dialogues with NGOs and any others with an interest in your company?

- Do your organizational narrative, facts, and Q&As need updating before something happens?

- Are you able to reach key constituents in the first hours of a crisis (such as getting mobile phone numbers in advance of when you might need them)?
- Are you prepared to use digital/mobile communication technologies to their full advantage?

Plugging a Leak (Literally)

An incident triggered by human error resulted in one of the most unexpected and bizarre public crises I have witnessed. I remember leaving a client's office in downtown Chicago after being told to evacuate the building. When I reached the street, I asked a police officer why the building was evacuated. It was a sunny spring morning, so I was puzzled to hear him respond using the word *flood*. He explained: "It's underground in the sub-basements of buildings in the Loop. It's coming from the river."

It turned out that public works employees had been driving new pylons next to a bridge where the Chicago River branches north. This was to protect against barges and river boats hitting and damaging the bridge structure. What the workers may not have realized was that there was an old underground tunnel system beneath the riverbed.

The tunnel system dated to the early 1900s. Over the years it had been used for underground telephone cables and as a delivery network for transporting supplies to restaurants and office buildings. Most Chicagoans had no idea the tunnel was even there.

It turned out that the workers driving the new pylons broke open a major hole that grew bigger as the river water rushed in and created a vortex, like water draining in a bathtub. The water poured into the underground tunnel system at the rate of hundreds of thousands of gallons an hour, flooding office basements throughout the city's most expensive real estate, affecting computer servers, telephone transmission cables, stored merchandise, and vital paper records.

Chicago's mayor was Richard M. Daley, the son of a legendary longtime Chicago mayor, and at the time in his third year in office. Can you imagine being the mayor of a great city, one that had survived the cataclysmic fire of 1871, and being told that your river was leaking? Daley would not be blamed if he had channeled his late father for advice in such an unusual situation. How do you fix a leak in the bottom of an urban river? Someone's initial quick fix of stuffing mattresses to plug the leak did not work very well.

The mayor quickly organized a team of public safety officials, federal authorities, and civil engineers to address the crisis before downtown Chicago became the first city to be destroyed by fire in one century and floodwaters in the next. In the end, thanks to the efforts of Kenny Construction Company and other problem solvers, the hole in the river was plugged. The estimated damage in terms of property and business revenue was put at more than one billion dollars.

Could any mayor anticipate and be ready to respond to a crisis like this? I would argue yes. In years since, we have seen mayors, governors, and other public officials prepare for both the imponderable and the predictable, with some inevitably performing better than others. While a leak in the Chicago River caught Daley off guard, he did the right thing in immediately surrounding himself with experts who could fix the hole.

Ducking the Problem

Experts say that in the age of artificial intelligence, computer programs can now generate thousands of risk-scenario patterns in a matter of seconds, everything from credit risk to cyberattacks. The programs, however, are created by humans who must anticipate the most likely crises by analyzing scenarios and coding the best preventive solutions, often with the help of cognitive computing.

This raises an organizational behavior question. Managers and employees know that it may be the correct and moral decision to expose potential problems. They also know that such information can be damaging to the firm if it ever comes to light. And that is the dilemma. In divulging such information to superiors, the consequences could affect the divulger's bottom line, his or her standing in the organization, and any future investment in their operations. All of which can be disincentives to expose risks.

It's not easy to blow the whistle on your own company's vulnerabilities. It's only human to keep bad news from supervisors for as long as possible. Some individuals try to handle the problem as is expected of a professional; others would rather leave the firm or be reassigned, leaving behind a big problem for someone else to deal with. That can turn out to be a very dangerous situation.

Remember when the Sony-supplied lithium-ion batteries in Dell laptop computers were catching fire in 2006? Ultimately, more than four million Dell laptops and notebooks were recalled. Sony's global CEO at the time, Howard

Stringer, did not learn of the severity of the problem until he received a call directly from Michael Dell, who is said to have asked Stringer, "What's wrong with those batteries you are supplying us?" (Or words to that effect.)

Reportedly, Stringer's managers at Sony had failed to report the bad news before it escalated into a full-blown crisis. What had to make it even more embarrassing for Stringer was that he had previously reached out to Dell for advice when he was considering taking on the role of a global CEO.

The problem? Stringer was trying to solve a major business issue—a battery problem—while working within a foreign company culture. Sony was a Japanese conglomerate, one with a highly siloed engineering culture that was significantly different from the ones he had experienced earlier in his career at CBS and Sony Corporation of America.

As Stringer told Mark Singer, a reporter for the *New Yorker,* a few months before the Sony battery crisis, "I'm very happy to delegate. Unlike many executives, I really do rely upon people who know a lot more than I do. I'm very careful to surround myself with people who fill in a lot of the blanks. I didn't go to school in management. I never wanted to bloody well *be* a manager."

Which might explain why Stringer was caught off guard when the laptop crisis hit. And that can happen.

Too many hours can pass before CEOs and leaders are apprised of situations that mark the start of a crisis. Today, that delay can be cut to mere minutes given how quickly the news of an accident or disaster makes its way to headquarters. But a creeping crisis can take much longer to reach the corner office.

Which is why a feedback loop is needed between the C-suite and employees.

Once informed, however, a leader who thinks an issue will fade away or never resurface is making a big mistake. Here's an example: a creative director at an advertising agency emailed employees and other guests an invitation to the company's holiday "Ghetto Party." According to an article in the *Wall Street Journal*, "the email included the picture of two African American men and called for 'ghetto music, Malt 45s at lunch, ghetto terminology, and of course, drugs and prostitutes are legal all day until close of business.'"

Not surprisingly, that email eventually was shared with an online reporter, who published it, triggering other business reporters to cover it, too. The ad agency lost its biggest client, and the CEO—who allegedly knew about the party and the denigrating nature of the email—was fired by his holding company. It was an ignominious end to a twenty-five-year career with his agency. A tough way to go out for someone who had the reputation of being a great salesman and business builder. (To its credit, the holding company that owns the agency appeared to act quickly in firing one of its top producers.)

That's how these stories end when a leader is slow to deal with a potentially incendiary situation. The people who conceived of the party and sent the email were no doubt jettisoned, too—yet another example of how really terrible judgment can cost people their jobs, reputations, and sometimes even their careers.

Assess Your Readiness

Sensitivity training could have helped prevent such crises. That's why I believe a company's cultural values need to be reinforced regularly. Crisis-preparation plans are important, but odds are they end up forgotten, archived on a computer, or filed in a desk drawer. More important than any plan is a mind-set to stay ever vigilant about potentially harmful issues.

For leaders trying to get ahead of the risk curve, it is best to start by assessing your organization, the operations, processes, policies, rules, exceptions, competitive and external threats, and the readiness of executives to avert major problems.

Ask yourself: What do you think can turn into something that can become much worse if it isn't fixed soon? This is similar to a patient examination conducted by a thorough physician. My doctor asks questions to identify current or future pain points. He takes note of what I tell him, coaxing more information from me. In doing so, he gets a better all-round picture of my health while diagnostic testing—blood labs, EKGs, and other tests—provides the benchmark data for annual re-evaluation.

Risk prevention and investigation should start with a lot of one-on-one conversations with people in charge of major functions. People generally don't like to bring up issues among colleagues, and that's part of the problem.

That's where my journalism training helped while engaging executives in corporate risk-management planning. I know how to put people at ease and get them to discuss things they might not initially want to talk about. After an hour-long conversation, I might finally get the person to say, "You know, this is what really keeps me up at three in the morning." That's when you start getting at some of the potential threats lurking below the surface.

Cross communication among departments and practices is also important to risk management. Information about issues is so often decentralized, if not buried, in departments. The dots cannot be connected until someone pieces it all together and sees the threat or problem in all its dimensions.

People in my business discipline—communications, marketing, brand people, public affairs—must continually engage with the rest of the organization in as many ways as possible. Too often we find out about crucial issues after the fact. To be more effective, we need a seat at the CEO's conference table and in the boardroom, or in executive committees with the CEO. We need to be part of those mission-critical conversations early on.

Communication executives and top consultants have to be part of the solution, part of the risk-management team dealing with issues before they become much larger problems.

Otherwise they are the people who get the call from the CEO or general counsel's office saying, "We've got a big problem and we need you to help fix it!"

Keep Your Antennae Tuned

Control Risks, a London-based specialist risk consultancy, has been in business more than forty years helping organizations deal with common geopolitical concerns: terrorism, unfair or corrupt trade practices, onerous regulations, hostile countries and markets, and natural and human-provoked disasters.

In its annual "RiskMap" study, Control Risks highlighted five top geopolitical risks on its 2019 watch list: China–U.S. trade confrontations and their global implications; conflicting regional data regulation policies; political gridlock at the federal level in the U.S.; extreme weather disruption; and nationless globalized companies against a backdrop of growing nationalism. I found this last risk intriguing.

The Control Risks report said that multinationals "risk—ironically—becoming nationless as nationalist politics continue to advance around the world. Formal and informal barriers are rising. Frictionless trade is beginning to rub, supply chains are starting to drag. Business leaders must re-calibrate and adapt to this new reality or global players will end up being played by a world in uncertain transition."

Leaders have enough continuing issues to worry about. "New realities" provide even greater challenges, as Control Risks and other observers see it.

Through their internal and external public affairs networks, companies (as well as NGOs) must keep their intelligence antennae tuned to warning signs of trouble. Leaders are surrounded by people with information and insights. They need to keep these people on their toes so that the organization can maintain a state of high alert and readiness.

For example, the communications team can design and operate a virtual situation room to monitor both the organization's intelligence sources and current events in real time. Data analysts can study and identify patterns in everything from social media chatter to what front-line company employees are seeing (sales associates) or hearing (customer service centers) to determine what merits increased corporate attention.

Communication and marketing executives are often at the

wellhead of myriad sources of data. Some problems can be hidden or obscured by data. And some may not even be in the data. We all know that it is not about big data or little data but *directional data*—well-examined insights that help focus corporate resources and actions that really matter.

As expectations seem to steadily rise in the capitalist world, companies need to be ever aware of dissatisfied shareholders. Hostile shareholder activism reached record levels in 2018 across the Americas and Europe and became more prevalent in Asia. Companies perceived as underperforming were targeted by Elliott Management, Carl Icahn, and other activist institutional investors aiming to change leadership and boards as a means to better corporate performance and value creation for shareholders.

Operational vs. Reputational Risk

One distinction I want to make, even though they are related, is that *there is a difference between business operational risk and reputational risk*. That being said, an unresolved operational risk can easily become a reputational risk.

I've worked with clients, including communications executives, who have been very savvy about this distinction. When presented with some new issue at their company, they say, "Okay, let's run through some scenarios. Here's the reputational risk if we do this—and here's the business risk, as well as the business opportunity." That's an important balancing act, because sometimes hidden in a problem is also an opportunity, just like the Chinese yin and yang. The question then becomes: Is the organization willing to risk its reputation for what could be a considerable business opportunity?

From One Crisis to Two

If you're in the freight rail business and there are fuel or gas pipelines running along the easements next to railway tracks, it would be wise to anticipate a potentially incendiary problem. I was involved in just such a situation, one that escalated from one crisis into two, when a train derailment that took place fifty miles east of Los Angeles led to a second incident twelve days later.

The first involved a runaway Southern Pacific freight train that derailed in San Bernardino after taking a curve at too high a speed. Four people—the conductor, another train employee, and two residents—were killed in the crash, and a row of houses in a lower-middle-class neighborhood was demolished. In the aftermath and cleanup, heavy earth-moving equipment inadvertently damaged a gasoline pipeline, producing a leak that went undetected.

According to the *New York Times*, "a gasoline pipeline under the accident site sprang a leak and exploded, killing two more people and burning down 10 more houses in the stricken neighborhood. Residents said they saw a spray of white fumes rise from the embankment below the tracks at about 8 A.M., and then a blast shook the area as an earthquake would. Billowing flames shot 300 feet into the warm morning air. Fire was coming down the street house to house."

The refined-fuel pipeline, known as the Cal-Nev Pipeline, runs more than five hundred miles from Nevada to Los Angeles and its ports. Cal-Nev executives rushed to the site and tried to calm the angry and aggrieved community. My firm at the time, GolinHarris, sent two of our best crisis managers—Richard Kline and Fred Cook (who would later become CEO of Golin)—to help manage the crisis at ground zero, which they did expertly under the circumstances. I stayed in Chicago and worked with the parent company, GATX.

GATX's CEO became quite anxious during a special board meeting to discuss the crisis. He asked for a detailed plan of action for bringing closure. I remember sketching out the plan in the GATX office while they were meeting, which helped to reduce some of the board's anxiety. But my colleagues Cook and Kline then did the heavy lifting over the course of weeks at the community level in California. And they did a great job.

I recall hearing about a reporter who asked a local official why the pipeline and the railroad tracks were located just fifty feet away from homes. The answer was to the effect that pipelines run through poorer communities because wealthier people don't want them in their neighborhoods.

Exactly. You're less likely to find gasoline pipelines running alongside railway tracks in high-end communities. Given this vulnerability, however, it does not really matter through which types of communities these rail lines and pipelines run. Accidents happen. Good risk management dictates that executives must game out all the scenarios in advance.

Think Like a Retailer

Keeping in mind my earlier commandment that you can make friends and allies only before a crisis—not during one—risk management requires companies to build relationships at the local level. That means initiating relationships with mayors, public safety officials, legislators, community and civic leaders, news media, and any others a company would be likely to deal with during a major incident.

No matter what type of company you are, you have to think like a retailer, or at least like someone who is engaged in the community. I'm not suggesting that you're going to have relationships with everyone, but you must establish them wherever you are most vulnerable. The best companies, especially industrial, energy, and transportation firms, conduct drills and initiate mock crises on a regular basis, often in conjunction with local public safety agencies. The drills include company executives who would be involved in addressing an actual incident. I've been involved in some of those drills, including a few where the scenarios were conducted in real time over the course of a few days, as if an accident had really just happened.

I've spent most of my career in an industry known as public relations, even though I view it much more broadly as encompassing communications of all kinds. Public relations in general is misunderstood, both as an industry and a term.

People use *PR* as a verb or a noun—that you're going to PR your way out of a problem, or that someone is just using PR to spin something. The *R* in PR is really about relationships: human relationships, institutional relationships, business-to-government relationships, business-to-NGO relationships. When an organization has a problem that results in loss of life, business disruption, inconvenience to customers, or loss of reputation, it quickly discovers the value of its public relationships.

Hank Paulson once said that his relationships with financial institution leaders, central bankers, and political leaders were crucial during the 2008 financial crisis. "Getting anything done requires working with others," he said. "It's all about personal relationships."

When I was the general manager of my firm's Chicago office, I believed that I needed to mobilize communication specialists if a client had an immediate crisis. And I learned from experience that a client's call for help could come at any time, day or night, weekend or holiday. I thus tried to train as many people in the office as I could in the basic strategies and skills of crisis containment. My thinking was that even those on my team with no prior experience could still help staff a crisis communication team if they possessed a basic understanding of what to do in a crisis.

To that end, we held a series of brown-bag training sessions for the professional staff on the ABCs of effective crisis management. Days after the third such session, I was at my desk, preparing for an important client meeting later that afternoon. A colleague in St. Louis called and said his client, an oil refiner, needed immediate help.

"How immediate?" I asked.

"Like ten minutes ago," he answered. The company had a refinery in a Chicago suburb and there had just been an explosion. Could I go there as soon as possible with a team of people to help direct the communications?

I told him that I had an unbreakable commitment, but that I would assemble the best team I could and dispatch them to the scene as quickly as possible. It was lunchtime on a beautiful day, and the office was quiet. I grabbed all staff on hand and told an employee to get ready to go to the scene of the explosion and to bring her notes from our recent crisis-training sessions. I then sent a second person to find other key people, who were having lunch nearby.

Once at the refinery, my team got to work immediately, interacting with plant management, writing statements to share with the news media, and prepping a company spokesman for live and taped interviews with broadcast and newspaper reporters. At some point in the afternoon, our team leader called and suggested it wasn't necessary for me to come to the refinery after all. The team had the situation under control and had devised a game plan for the rest of the weekend.

Anticipating crises and preparing people to deal with them can make the difference between successful situational containment and bungled crisis management. To deal with big potential risks, first try to make an intelligent guess about what can happen, and then prepare for its likelihood. As a friend once said about riding motorcycles, "There are two types of motorcycle riders—those who have fallen and those who will fall."

Key Insights and Observations

- Unlike crisis management, which is largely reactive, risk management—with its goal of crisis anticipation and preparation—is a proactive process.
- Risk-taking can lead to great success, but risk-ignorance can result in costly failure. Big problems occur when smaller problems are neglected or do not receive leadership.

- Leaders cannot emphasize risk identification enough. They need to create an internal communication environment in which to identify risks before they intensify.
- The best way to stay ahead of the risk curve is to create a culture that encourages more active monitoring, discussion, and resolution of potential risks before they turn into crises.
- Preventing bad things from happening does not get rewarded enough by board directors, shareholders, voters, and others who ultimately judge a leader's performance.

"Let's change 'brink of chaos' to 'Everything is wonderful.'"

5

Sizzle to the Narrative

"The more elaborate our means of communication, the less we communicate."

—**Joseph Priestley,** eighteenth-century scientist and discoverer of oxygen

In the movie *The Formula,* Marlon Brando played a 1970s-era American oil titan, a character said to be loosely modeled on Dr. Armand Hammer of Occidental Petroleum. The conspiracy thriller did poorly among reviewers and at the box office, but it did produce some memorable dialogue. At one point in the film, a business crony, arguing that "PR is right," tells Brando's CEO character that a gasoline price hike can work. "We can blame it on the Arabs," he suggests. Brando's character responds dismissively: "Arthur, you are missing the point—we *are* the Arabs."

At least Brando's industry leader did not blame the problem on bad public relations. He was quite aware of his industry's reputational issues at a time of conspiracy theories about oil price manipulation. My point? Leaders should not blame the communications team when their companies and industries come under public scrutiny and fire. (Unless, of course, their PR people are myopic or inept.) Because leaders have a responsibility—fiduciary and otherwise—to both promote and safeguard the reputations of their enterprises.

If you are the founder and your name is on the door, it is even more important that you take a crucial role in shaping how your brand is viewed by customers, potential employees, business regulators, and other key audiences. Advertising legend Leo Burnett reportedly exclaimed, "Take my name off the door!" whenever he saw his eponymous firm producing mediocre advertising unworthy of the firm's and his personal reputation.

If a leader's communication is not perceived as strategic, dynamic, and credible, and in sync with brand aspirations and message platforms, the organization will suffer. But the messaging must come from many minds. Large organizations today have hundreds of people employed at storytelling, branded content, paid and earned media, data analytics, audience engagement, and a plethora of distribution methods through news media and social platforms.

Narrative Leaders

If a leader isn't happy with the organization's narrative content, he or she should meet with the communications and marketing teams and discuss how to make it better. The quest for better content can also lead to questions about how the organization can improve its products and services, which ultimately leads—in a virtuous circle—to better, unified narrative content.

Even though most business schools do not emphasize communication as an executive educational priority, the newest generation of leaders seems to better understand the importance of communication in all they do. At the same time, while young entrepreneurial leaders may be digital natives, that does not necessarily mean they are all good communicators. They must work at it, too.

Gen X and baby boomer leaders have adapted to the social media age (in some cases thanks to millennial mentoring). They regularly communicate digitally with their social-savvy children and grandchildren, and it's routine today for parents and grandparents to text, send emojis, and engage on Snapchat and Instagram. Leaders today should recognize that there are so many ways to reach people with messaging directly through their own organizations and through third parties and social influencers.

Which means that leaders have the means and also the ability to deliver and reinforce timely messages to thousands if not millions of people. Oprah Winfrey has more than forty-two million followers on Twitter. Pope Francis has almost eighteen million followers. The Dalai Lama has nineteen million. Those numbers pale in comparison to President Donald Trump's nearly sixty million followers (compared to Vladimir Putin's seven hundred thousand, probably consisting of bots). Or former President Barack Obama's more than one hundred million.

Leaders have had to balance one of the greatest responsibilities of modern management: adopting modern technologies that replace human labor while trying to retrain and repurpose the people in their organizations that the new machines and processes replace. This is occurring in companies of all types as they adapt to data-driven business models fueled by artificial intelligence (AI) and mobile technology. Ever since the sixteenth century, technology has been revolutionizing mass communication. The speed of sophisticated omnichannel platforms and distribution systems of today enable the frequent leadership messaging that provides big-picture enterprise context. Yet there are no algorithms or machine-learning capabilities I know of that can provide leaders with all of the right words and messages, conveyed at the right time and to ensure receptivity. Then again, maybe the Alexa of leadership communication is coming soon.

Publicis Groupe is one global communications firm that has taken AI very seriously with substantial research and investments. Speaking at a major conference in India, Guillaume Herbette, CEO of Publicis Groupe's MSLGroup, explained that companies need to embrace artificial intelligence and other new immersive technologies.

"AI combines the best of science and technology with storytelling. It will change the way we work," Herbette said. "It is not possible to stop the revolution."

He said that AI applications for business were expected to grow by 300 percent worldwide, creating business worth $1.2 trillion by 2019. Companies deepening their use of AI and sophisticated data analytics would be the greatest beneficiaries. "The era of augmented influence is upon us," Herbette said. "Technology is increasingly mixing with our reality in both positive and negative ways. Transformation and adaptation is required by everyone."

The world is hyperconnected, with the only limitation being the possible bandwidth of internet and Wi-Fi providers as billions of global users spend hours each day online, uploading and downloading terabytes of information and entertainment. So far, no one has really "broken" the internet.

A Climate of Trust

I have come to know many capable communicators who truly understand the high responsibility of leadership communication and have served chief executives well. Bill Margaritis is one of them. A veteran corporate communications professional who spent much of his career at FedEx, he worked closely with its founder and longtime CEO, Frederick Smith, who has been recognized as one of the ablest of corporate leaders.

"A leader ... needs to inspire and motivate people to achieve their full potential," Margaritis said in a speech to public relations professionals. "They need to have a clear and compelling vision for the team, think ahead and anticipate trends, build the right chemistry, culture, and values, and have a broad view of the world they operate in. And most importantly, a good leader establishes a climate of trust among team members and an *all for one, one for all* mind-set."

The Walmart Way

Frequent, mission-driven communication is one of a leader's best weapons for getting people to buy in to a dream, to get everyone on the same page, and to redirect an organization in ways that will allow it to perform better.

Appealing to workers' personal pride and collective esteem is as important as the message itself. Sam Walton, who founded Walmart, one of the biggest companies in the world, put it another way: "Outstanding leaders go out of their way to boost the self-esteem of their personnel. If people believe in themselves, it's amazing what they can accomplish."

In his book *Made in America,* Walton once listed his ten rules on leading and building a business, half of them specifically relating to best practices in leadership communication. Walton preached:

- Motivate your partners. Money and ownership alone are not sufficient.
- Communicate everything you possibly can to your partners. The more they know...the more they will care.
- Appreciate everything your associates do for the business... Nothing can substitute for a few well-chosen and well-timed, sincere words of praise.
- Celebrate your success and find some humor in your failures. Have fun and show enthusiasm always.
- Listen to everyone in your company and figure out ways to get them talking.

Sam Walton definitely had good business instincts. He also had emotional intelligence (EI) at a time when EI wasn't talked about.

The instinctive part of leadership communication likely depends in part on emotional intelligence, according to Travis Bradberry, cofounder of TalentSmart and an expert on the subject of EI. "Great communicators inspire people," he wrote in a *Forbes* commentary. "They create a connection that is real, emotional, and personal. And great communicators forge this connection through an understanding of people and an ability to speak directly to their needs in a manner that they are ready to hear."

The CEO of Microsoft agrees. "I think EQ is more important than IQ for a leader," said Satya Nadella to a business audience. He also talked about clarity of purpose, collaboration, and empathy as being critical to establish trust in the leader.

I like what Margaritis said about creating an institutional "climate of trust." Communication in so many ways is about establishing trust—and trust in an organization starts at the top. **The leader therefore must be the chief credibility officer.** This principle applies whether the organization is a family business, a board of education, or even the White House. Especially the White House.

I recall a discussion about credibility with a group of Saudi Arabian ministry heads when my agency team traveled to Riyadh to pitch a multifaceted, global communications program for a new Saudi government initiative called the King Abdullah City for Atomic and Renewable Alternative Energy (known as KA-CARE).

At the end of our fast-paced thirty-minute presentation, one of the lead ministers asked, "If you believe we have a good reputation today, then why do we need your firm?" A good question after we had praised the ministers for their bold and important plans.

"I learned this in journalism school: if your mother tells you she loves you, check it out!" I replied to the minister. I was seated next to a colleague who was a former political reporter for an American newspaper. I immediately sensed his nervousness about me using an old journalism adage to address the minister's question.

But I knew immediately that the Saudis were puzzled by my remark. I quickly added context, arguing that some critics and opinion leaders would likely think the real purpose of the Saudi government's new alternative energy program would be to develop nuclear weapons. The KA-CARE program would need to respond to and withstand considerable skepticism—if not cynicism—from government officials and news media in Washington, DC, London, Tel Aviv, and many other capitals.

Skeptical observers would want to verify—to "check it out"—before trusting that the stated purpose behind the alternative energy project was indeed legitimate.

After a long pause, the Saudi minister who had asked the initial question began to laugh, now understanding my "if your mother tells you she loves you" point. The other Saudis began to laugh as well. A few days later we learned that we had won the assignment to work on the launch of KA-CARE, which included communication targeted toward persuading the skeptical. Of course, fast-forwarding, trust of the Saudi government suffered terribly after the murder of Saudi journalist Jamal Khashoggi, darkening the reputation of Crown Prince Mohammed bin Salman.

As leaders build the narratives for their organizations, they will never convince everyone. For there will always be news reporters and commentators who are cynical about specific companies or entire industries.

Here's an example: when retiring Exxon CEO Rex Tillerson appeared before a U.S. Senate committee prior to his eventual confirmation as U.S. Secretary of State, Holman W. Jenkins Jr. of the *Wall Street Journal* wrote the following about the hearing and the oil industry: "When senators aren't bashing Mr. T [Tillerson] over Russia, they are likely to bash him over climate change. But several common mistakes are illustrated in this indictment. It makes no sense for a company whose expertise is oil geology to invest in wind or solar, very different skill sets. Oil companies do so only for PR reasons—so they can decorate their annual reports with windmills and solar panels."

Assuming an industry leader doesn't take the cynical attitude about PR as the Brando character did in *The Formula,* he can play a significant role in shaping a credible organizational narrative. James Mulva did it with town hall–style community meetings when he was CEO of ConocoPhillips. And Robert Dudley has been doing it at BP, repairing its reputation since taking over the chief leadership role in the aftermath of the Deepwater Horizon accident and ensuing crisis.

What specifically should leaders do to be active communicators, both inside and outside the enterprise? Some answers are obvious:

- Make sure you are talking to or meeting with customers frequently, in addition to what customer-relationship executives and managers are already doing.
- Stay in touch with major shareholders and credit holders.
- Use interviews with securities analysts and reporters to drive home the key messages of the organizational

narrative, but also to learn about developing trends or competitive initiatives.

- Become active on social networks (with the help of your social media ninjas).
- Use video content to let employees and other stakeholders see and hear from you more often.

Overcommunicating is necessary, as Jack Welch suggested, so that specific messages get across. Political campaigns overcommunicate all the time based on the standard industry belief that people must view a political commercial at least seven times before they begin to truly remember it.

CNBC has conducted research that backs the network's claim that CEOs interviewed most often on its business and markets-focused programs are viewed more favorably than those who aren't. Is it that they seem likable given their many on-air appearances? Or is it because they become more familiar through the repetition of messages and appearances?

Experience has shown that institutional investors expect corporate leaders to have a communicative management style and to view transparency as good corporate governance. The 2017 "Report from the Buy Side," conducted by global PR agency Weber Shandwick in partnership with KRC Research, found that nearly four out of five investors said they were inclined to pay additional attention to CEO actions during times of financial difficulty or in the face of a public image crisis.

The study noted that "investors consider their personal interactions with the C-suite to be critical in making investment decisions. Investors would like to interact with senior management on average seven times per year."

Crisis or no crisis, leaders committed to a robust organizational narrative should periodically review what the organization is doing with respect to all vital communications. And not just when it comes to advertising, which because of the size of ad expenditures usually gets the leader's attention, even more when the advertising is judged to be ineffective. That means reviewing the outlays and outcomes of all corporate, product, social, and audience-specific communications.

The Power of a Good Story

In 2016, the faculty at the Medill School of Journalism, Media, Integrated Marketing Communications at Northwestern, my graduate school alma mater, taught a class called Leadership Communication for Maximum Impact: Storytelling. It was described in the course catalogue thusly: "Storytelling is an essential part of leadership. Effective leaders communicate to inspire talent to excel; to partner with investors and communities; to engage with customers and clients to grow their impact in the world as part of a global community. Cultivating an authentic, trustworthy, and compelling narrative is vital to a leader's success."

If you study leaders who have been effective communicators, you are likely to find that many are good at telling stories. The best stand-up comedians and paid dinner speakers know this. David Rubenstein gets it. He is a founder and former co-CEO of the Carlyle Group, one of the largest private equity and asset management firms in the world. He is also a major philanthropist and has hosted for years a Bloomberg television program dedicated to interviewing other business and government leaders and leaders in the arts and sciences.

A few years ago, Rubenstein was the featured speaker at the Economic Club of Chicago. Instead of speaking from a podium at the center of the dais, as most speakers before him had done, Rubenstein walked out onto a makeshift stage positioned in front of the dais. For the next twenty minutes, he delivered to the thousand or so guests a monologue equal to any late-night talk show host. He spoke quickly, delivering line after witty line and pausing occasionally for effect.

He received a standing ovation before sitting down for a moderated question session in which he continued to entertain and illuminate the audience.

Rubenstein recounted the story of discovering that one of only seventeen known copies of the 1215 Magna Carta was to be auctioned by Sotheby's. It was the only privately owned copy, having once been owned by billionaire businessman Ross Perot. (The other sixteen original copies were in British museums and institutions.) Rubenstein acquired the document and donated it to the U.S. National Archives as a "down payment on my obligation to give back to the country."

Asked that evening if he was willing to admit any investment mistakes he had made at Carlyle, Rubenstein mentioned two, both doozies. The first, he said, was when his son-in-law wanted to introduce him to a former classmate from Phillips Exeter Academy who had a business investment idea. "Companies that deal with college-related things, they never really make it," Rubenstein said. "I have seen these companies over the years, so I told him I was not interested in meeting or investing." He then added that his son-in-law's friend happened to be a guy named Mark Zuckerberg.

Rubenstein then told the audience a story of being introduced to an emerging entrepreneur who wanted to purchase the rights to a book collection owned by one of Carlyle's portfolio companies. The entrepreneur was willing to offer a third of his company's ownership in exchange for the books, but Rubenstein turned him down. That man was Jeff Bezos. He said he later went back to Bezos and was able to negotiate a 1 percent interest in Amazon, which eventually was worth several billion dollars.

A few weeks after that appearance, I met Rubenstein briefly at his Washington, DC, office and complimented him on how people at the Economic Club dinner were still talking about his remarks. "They must have low standards in Chicago," he wryly replied.

Rubenstein isn't the only well-known business leader who knows the power of storytelling. Another is Virgin Group founder Richard Branson, who once said in a *Forbes* interview, "Today, if you want to succeed as an entrepreneur, you also have to be a good storyteller." Paul Polman, the longtime chief executive of Unilever, shared that sentiment, noting that "we do a lot of storytelling" at Unilever to achieve breakthrough cerebral and heartfelt consumer connections to the company's brands.

Branson belongs to that rare company of leaders whose organizations have grown and prospered as the leader became a cultural icon as well as the primary storyteller. The difference between Branson and Polman is that Branson is a celebrity showman and Virgin's storyteller in chief, and always has been. Polman operated as part of a team in crafting Unilever's corporate narrative, sharing the storytelling with many others.

"Mr. Virgin" has always been fond of publicity stunts. After establishing successful businesses including Virgin Atlantic

Airlines and Virgin Mobile, a wireless service, in 1994 Branson entered the beverage industry with the launch of Virgin Cola. To promote the new brand, he drove a small tank over cases of Coca-Cola in New York's Times Square. (The stunt received great publicity, but ultimately Virgin Cola never threatened the top cola brands. Branson would later tell *Forbes* that his assault on the cola industry was perhaps his biggest "flop.")

Storyteller in Chief

Celebrities representing brands in commercials today are no longer just spokespersons. Some, like Reese Witherspoon in her work with Elizabeth Arden, have been elevated to the role of storyteller in chief. In a statement to *People* magazine in 2017, Witherspoon referred to herself as a creative partner to the Elizabeth Arden brand team, "highlighting female-centric stories that illustrate women's true-life experiences, which unite us all."

Elizabeth Arden's president at the time, JuE Wong, described Witherspoon as someone well connected with target consumers. "Her authenticity, which resonates worldwide, combined with her business acumen, digital prowess, and social media footprint, provide a unique opportunity to further develop the 'Liz Arden persona,' connect with women, and inspire them to go out and 'make their mark.'"

In other words, the Elizabeth Arden brand bet big on the ability of a well-known celebrity to build the brand. It will be interesting to see how much Witherspoon's role actually goes beyond telling the Arden story in thirty-second videos posted on YouTube and other social media sites.

Not many people or companies have that storyteller in chief title yet. Can the head of a major nation be a storyteller in chief? Xi Jinping, president of the People's Republic of China, is one, according to an American journalist.

"To Xi Jinping's growing list of titles as *Chairman of Everything*, add one more: Storyteller-in-Chief," wrote China-based David Bandurski in the *Los Angeles Review of Books*. He went on to describe the many books that President Xi had published since becoming general secretary of the Chinese Communist Party in 2012.

He said Xi's goal was to of use China's soft power to make its story more compelling to the world. Bandurski further noted that "As China's top leader and chief messenger, Xi Jinping is the custodian of the 'China story'—the authorized version of how the country and its leadership wish to be perceived."

Bandurski is no state-sponsored publicist for Xi. A graduate, like me, of the Medill School, he is co-director of the China Media Project. He received a Human Rights Press Award in 2007 for an explanatory article about China's internet censorship guidelines. While Bandurski notes that some of Xi's books have not sold well outside China, there is no question that Xi has gotten traction with his nationalistic narrative about China's twenty-first-century destiny as a global power. He speaks all around the world while his government censors free speech and restricts independent political and social thought in his country.

As the *Economist* observed about Xi as he consolidated power: "Xi is determined to reimpose discipline on a querulous society that in recent years, thanks to the rapid spread of social media, has become much better equipped to organize itself independently of the party and to evade official controls."

Storytelling in all of its rhetorical and literary appeal, however, should not be confused with journalism, despite the old saw that some journalists never let the facts get in the way of a good story. Journalism is the gathering, editing, and presentation of news and information through media. Its twenty-first-century transmedia formats and platforms may be different, but it is still subject to the same standards of integrity that have held firm over the past few centuries. "I think the fundamentals of journalism remain the same," CBS Evening News Anchor Norah O'Donnell told *Parade* magazine. "They go back to truth and trust, and that we are journalists reporting instead of storytelling."

Broadcast journalists have the advantage of telling stories primarily through high-definition video and infographics. We live in a highly visual world for both the literate and illiterate. There are still significant parts of the world where indigenous peoples respond best—as their ancient ancestors did—to visual communication. If you have traveled through such nations, you will see communication in the form of large pictures painted on buildings.

Storytelling and narrativity have an important place in organizational and personal life. As members of communities, as citizens in a democracy, and as colleagues in a business or other type of organization, storytelling matters. Storytelling connects people to each other, to ideas, to higher values and standards of excellence. Communication technology enables us to tell our stories one to one, or one to millions. But it also poses challenges and risks, due in part to the speed at which communication travels today.

Even in the highly literate world, visual information is the most effective form of *misinformation.* It travels faster than truth. Global social platforms such as Facebook are increasingly confronting this problem, and as a result, rethinking their news feeds. Even as Facebook founder and CEO Mark Zuckerberg has steered clear of taking corporate responsibility for the platform's considerable role in the spread of misinformation, the company is working to figure out how to minimize the damage caused by "fake news"—Russia's meddling in the 2016 U.S. presidential election being a prime example.

Nobody Knows Your Story Better

I have been storytelling since Nixon was president. I have studied and practiced communication since I was a teenager writing for my hometown newspaper. Early in my career, I was a multimedia journalist (print and broadcast) before the term *multiplatform* had even been coined. Had social media channels been available in my early journalism days, I would have enthusiastically embraced them to target and build broad audiences for my stories, just as clever journalists do today.

When it comes to storytelling, leaders should adopt the principle I have practiced throughout my career: nobody can tell your story better than you. Who and what fills the void if you are not telling your own story?

Unless, of course, you are totally inept at storytelling. How many times have you tried to tell a good story you heard from a parent, sibling, or business associate, only to leave out essential details or botch the punchline? Frustrated, we often turn to the original storyteller and say, "C'mon, you tell it. It's your story."

Of course, the person who lived the story remembers it best, often as if it were yesterday, and knows how to pace it, what to emphasize, and how to finish with gusto.

I've always found it astounding that old-school leaders of generations past didn't get this basic best practice for telling their own story, instead believing it was better to say little or nothing and assume people would reach the right conclusion on their own. That was common practice back in the day. Just make and sell a great product or service and your reputation will take care of itself. Some leaders believed advertising was all you needed to connect an organization with customers and other key audiences.

But advertising alone, even in large quantities, doesn't mean people are going to buy your product, or experience it in the ways your advertising suggests. Especially since the audience you are most trying to reach is increasingly fragmented across the modern media spectrum. Aggregating big audiences through what used to be called "mass communications" is much harder. Studies show that advertising is less memorable today, and perhaps even fraudulent in its digital formats, given how difficult it is to separate real consumers from internet bots. Placing ads programmatically, as it is called, is now done by computer programs.

Location, Location, Location

Where you tell your story is also important. More than 78 percent of those under age fifty get their news from social media sites, according to the Pew Research Center's 2017 American Trends Panel. More interestingly, more than half of all Americans over the age of fifty do, too. Online news has almost caught up with television as the number one source for news. That's both good and bad for leaders.

The good news is that if you are trying to engage the public—consumers, investors, followers, etc.—Facebook and other digital channels carry both influence and reach. Facebook has sucked up advertising dollars the way Amazon disrupted brick-and-mortar retailing. It and other social platforms reach people on their smartphones, on their laptops and tablets at work, while they are commuting—wherever they are. Digital reach is now ubiquitous.

On the other hand, newspapers and magazines continue to be the place for companies and newsmakers to tell their stories more fully. But newspaper and magazine circulations continue to decline each year, even if some newspapers have done well with online subscriptions and overall readership.

In fact, leaders who don't like journalists may enjoy the fact that their ranks are thinning: the American Society of News Editors reported that since 1994, newsrooms have lost more than twenty thousand jobs—more than 40 percent of their news staffs.

This is a terrible trend, particularly for those who have a story to be told in depth and with proper context in a print or long-form format. Television news, particularly the local variety, has been dumbed down. Tweets, out-of-context statements, and weather updates drive entire cycles in a quantity-over-quality news world. Similarly, many online news and infotainment sites resemble digital vending machines, offering some intellectual protein but a lot of sugary confectionaries, too.

We should not generalize that the twenty-first-century media behemoths like Facebook, Google, Disney, NewsCorp, and Viacom have taken all of the news media real estate. Corporations have become media publishers, even though they are not in the media business per se. There are tens of thousands of podcasters, bloggers, alternative media, and so-called citizen journalists out there. In some cities, ethnic media—in the form of physical newspapers and websites—abound.

But another viewpoint is that a glut of useless, purposeless information—words, pictures, infographics, videos—pours into pseudo-news websites like water rushing over Niagara Falls. The internet search engine "factories" in operation all around the world waste energy and result in a new kind of pollution: information and entertainment pollution disguised as a cacophony of choice. But this is the environment in which storytelling exists today.

Telling the complete story is important but difficult. It's not enough to just say, "We make a great product and you should buy it." Today, the story is as much about who makes the product as the product itself. Who are the people behind the product? Will it be good the next time I buy it? The story has to take into account other, equally important issues including supply chain, offshore sourcing of labor and raw materials, and other practices your customers are going to know and care about. At the same time, there is always information that companies need to hold back regarding product development, deals they are pursuing, internal tensions and politics, and other matters they prefer to keep private.

Earned vs. Paid Media

I believe that even in this era of 24-7 news and social media channels, you don't have to be out there talking about yourself all the time, even if you are a big global company. But you must be opportunistic, paying close attention to trend lines and current events, and pick spots where your perspective on a developing story—in or outside your industry—results in valuable visibility for your organization. This is known in the parlance of public relations as "earned media." It's earned because you did not have to buy it as you do with advertising (known as "paid media").

As a former journalist and successful PR representative, I spent a good portion of my early career assisting clients with earned media. Viewed as a go-to intermediary with reporters, my job was to help clients figure out how they could make their narratives more compelling to news organizations—and then go make it happen.

This meant working closely with subject-matter experts in my clients' organizations, developing what we thought were compelling stories, or contributing pieces for broader industry or trend stories. Each "storyline" or theme was supported by facts, research, government reports, anecdotes, visuals, and customer testimonials. Acting as an intermediary between the client and a news organization—a newspaper, magazine, TV network—I would pitch the stories to specific reporters and editors. Some of the reporters and editors knew me; many did not. Having been a reporter, however, I operated under the principle that I would never pitch a story idea that I would reject were I the reporter in question.

I made it a point to communicate the story idea in sixty seconds or less on a phone call, or in a few paragraphs in a letter (and in fewer words yet when the age of email became commonplace). While this practice is commonly known as media relations, I call it *media negotiations.* Relationships with news media professionals—as with any professionals—are important. But relationships, even friendships, won't get you a story if the reporter or editor is not impressed.

It still works if a person understands what journalists want and need to report their news and feature stories. Being a journalist-turned-media-relations pro helps, but the real skill is in research and creativity—researching topics and subject matter thoroughly across media with an eye toward finding story opportunities that have not yet been reported. In leadership communication, emotional intelligence and a little bit of heart complements rational arguments.

I've had clients look upon competitors' favorable media coverage with envy, especially when those competitors capitalized on or—even better—anticipated a trend and made themselves centerpieces of significant stories. They would say things like, "We should have been in that story in the *New York Times* or in *Fortune*," or "Why were we not in that nice piece on NBC seen by millions of people?" But the company had to figure out what their story was and put their confidence in people who could help them make those stories happen. In the old days, this was a form of media relations known as "placing stories." The best media relations occur when a reporter and PR representative find a place where their professional interests intersect.

Journalism's role in a complex democratic society is debated often today. Legendary Chicago newspaper editor and columnist Finley Peter Dunne once said that journalism's role was "meant to comfort the afflicted and afflict the comfortable." He also advised, "Trust everybody but cut the cards." Those two statements still tell us a great deal about modern journalists. They may be professionally skeptical, or even cynical, but more often than not they have a soft spot when it comes to helping to "comfort the afflicted." And they will expose any organization for inflicting pain or injustice on others if they can verify evidence to support it.

Leaders can expect to see some factual errors and misperceptions in the media about their organizations—or about them personally. These can come from customers, competitors, or even critics who don't, for whatever reason, like them. If misperceptions become more a pattern than an episodic annoyance, then it's a real problem. The best defense is to be well organized and ready to correct misinformation as quickly as possible.

Why do leaders need help from pros? A leader is wise to have a chief communications executive and team that is constantly studying the landscape for risks and time bombs; balancing brand and business-building opportunities against reputational risks; digging deep into the business to mine the best mosaic pieces for storytelling and narrative; adding value with key messages well delivered across a plethora of media channels; carefully reviewing the organization for any fractures in the desired culture; and snuffing out credibility-damaging brush fires.

Key Insights and Observations

- Leaders must accept some of the blame if the organizations they are leading are not getting good PR. Leaders of organizations have a responsibility—fiduciary and otherwise—to both promote and safeguard the reputations of their enterprises.

- The CEO must be the chief credibility officer. Communication in so many ways is about establishing trust—and trust in an organization starts at the top.
- When it comes to storytelling, leaders of organizations should adopt the principle I have practiced throughout my career. That is: nobody can tell your story better than you can.

"Thanks to our lightning-fast communications, we can now support an even larger, slower bureaucracy."

6

Leaders Need Communications Pros

"With the management turmoil we see within many corporations today, advising leaders on effective communication that employs all platforms and modern techniques is essential. The wise leaders will sit up and listen."

—Janet Robinson, former CEO,
The *New York Times* Company

Leaders are de facto chief credibility officers for their organizations. If the leader does not inspire trust and is not respected for his or her credibility, the image of the whole organization can suffer. They also must realize that an organization's communications are with human beings, and therefore must not be devoid of empathy and the right measure of emotion.

Able communicators know it takes a highly competent team to maximize their reach and effectiveness. The best leaders surround themselves with the best people, especially communication professionals. They also support the enabling technology and resources necessary to make leadership communication a strategic function in their organizations.

Frequently, C-suite and enterprise communication duties are the responsibility of a chief communications officer. This is a position that has become more influential in the twenty-first century as the communication needs of corporations and institutions grow increasingly global, complex, and immediate. In the best situations, chief communication officers have daily access to the leaders of their organizations, including the CEO, and work collaboratively with other functional leaders.

It is the CCO's job not only to worry about the organization's external reputation, but also to transcend barriers that often impede their colleagues from communicating effectively internally. They know that internal, connective dialogue can have a material impact on performance.

Leaders want to make their communications activities as efficient and impactful as possible. Every day. Because you don't have a lot of time to spend rewriting message points. You don't have time to waste while preparing for presentations or big-time media interviews.

Yes, you must prepare, but you have—or should have—people around you to help prepare you for those opportunities. You shouldn't expend too much of your precious energy and mental resources worrying in the middle of the night before a major communication event. Proper forethought helps avoid second-guessing afterward about how you could have communicated better and achieved a better outcome.

The communications chief is the person charged with opening clear channels of communication among the people who serve customers and other constituents every day.

"In our volatile and pugilistic world, with the democratization of brand via social media, uncertainty in politics and societies, and the transformation of journalism, smart leaders recognize that the CCO is a powerful partner in enhancing reputation, culture, and commercial success," wrote GE's Gary Sheffer in a *Fortune* commentary.

Sheffer, who was vice president of communications at General Electric until his retirement in 2015 and was well regarded by his corporate communications peers at other large companies, further noted that he "visited GE's employees all over the world to seek understanding about the company and to build trust with my colleagues. I needed to know how we made money, what data best illuminate our performance, and what big problems we were trying to solve. This helped our team to humanize the colossus that is GE."

No Yes-Men

An Egon Zehnder study of German CEOs validated the high premium leaders place on the crucial role played by their communication executives. According to the study, "without exception the CEOs questioned say that they want their CCO to be a kind of sparring partner. A solid basis of knowledge about the business is very important here. Only as an insider and an experienced manager in his or her own right would the CCO be in a position to offer advice to the CEO on an equal footing, and to develop and effectively represent an independent opinion. The CCO—say the CEOs—is a spokesperson, minister of external affairs and adviser.

Sometimes the CCO is even described as the CEO's alter ego. To fulfill this role effectively calls for a self-confident personality—ideally, perhaps, someone who is more extrovert by nature. The CEOs don't want 'yes men' as their CCOs—they want individuals who can contradict them and sometimes say 'no.'"

Steve Barrett, editor in chief of *PRWeek* U.S., put it well in saying, "While there is certainly a requirement for the modern CCO to completely embrace data, digital, social, and content in their skill set, the heavy lifting of reputation management and crisis response are still key tools in the armory—and CEOs rely on them for this."

Chief communications executives and their teams take on so many important responsibilities each day and throughout the year. Those include: overall content strategy; oversight of digital engagement systems; stakeholder relationship mapping; speeches and supporting logistics for the CEO and other executives; presentations at investment and industry conferences; message consistency, cadence, and alignment across audiences; development of communication plans to drive business transformation and change programs; preparing briefing books for board meetings; product launches and coordinated multichannel communication plans; and candid assessment of newly discovered corporate opportunities and risks.

And there's more: employee town hall meetings and live webcasts; opinions on community outreach and philanthropy; relationship-building activities and partnerships with media; employee advocacy programs; sponsorships and special events; precise wording and timing of policy decisions and announcements; monitoring Twitter, Facebook, and the growing array of other social media channels; responding rapidly to critical product reviews and customer complaints suggesting troubling patterns; input into customer communications, marketing programs, research interpretation and data analysis, and other written and verbal interactions with stakeholders; and coordination with the institution's experts dealing with government, NGOs, and public affairs.

One-off situations come up periodically as well, all of which makes zero-based budgeting nearly impossible for a major company's communications department. Faced with all these priorities and exigencies, the communications chief must take a deep breath and hope nothing blows up at work during family time. Whether or not it does, it's clear that the communications chief wears more hats than the crowd at England's Royal Ascot races on Ladies' Day.

In large organizations, many of the activities mentioned above might well show up on the agenda each and every day. I remember leading a project for Selim Bingol, then the chief communications executive at AT&T (before going on to work in a similar capacity at General Motors and Duke Energy). We examined and benchmarked the growing twenty-first-century responsibilities of CCOs and found "scope creep," meaning that more and more organizational responsibilities—communication related and otherwise—are being assigned to communications chiefs.

I have seen CCOs responsible for everything from trade show logistics to human resources to coordinating use of the corporate air fleet. No wonder leaders rely so heavily on communication chiefs like Bingol and their teams to always be on call—nights, weekends, and holidays. Their jobs are to make sure their organizations are firing on all cylinders and to bring the tangibly constructive and sometimes intangible value that good communication discipline and practices provide.

But an atmosphere of good organizational communication must start with the leader.

"CEOs should expect—and allow—senior communications executives to take a truly holistic approach to their jobs, with responsibility for assessing and helping to improve verbal and nonverbal communications throughout their organizations," wrote Walter Montgomery, former CEO of Robinson Lerer & Montgomery, in an article published in *Knowledge@Wharton.* "The lack of such comprehensive strategic oversight of the ways a company communicates results in unseen vulnerabilities, missed opportunities, and unfortunate surprises for senior management."

The Situation Room

That is why so many chief communication executives have become trusted sounding boards for leaders, especially in dealing with potential risks that could turn into much larger issues. First-class communication requires first-class resources such as:

- Experienced professionals in lead positions and roles, people who can build chemistry with the executive team and not be fearful of delivering constructive criticism and situational judgment when needed.

- Internal information systems that allow the comms team to interact easily and quickly with people and data from across the organization.
- Budgets shared with other functions to conduct communication training exercises for the leaders in the organizations, including one-on-one training for executives in need of communication skills updates.
- Situation rooms or designated places where social media practitioners can monitor all activity across social media communities on a 24-7 basis. These are ideal for daily business intelligence feeds, as well as for emergency purposes such as crisis situations and brand-recovery campaigns.

That last point is a key one. We live in a time when state leaders and their generals can watch war-zone battles live from their situation rooms. Major telecommunications companies such as AT&T have global network operation centers that resemble something out of NASA or NORAD. In these giant spaces, filled with floor-to-ceiling monitors and data screens, they can watch data, wireless, and all the 24-7 traffic on their networks.

These operations are too expensive and elaborate for most organizations, but they provide a glimpse of leading-edge technologies and what a future corporation "war room" or situation center might require for constant communication with its many spheres of influence.

Bill Margaritis, introduced earlier, held senior communication and marketing positions for FedEx, Bechtel, and Hilton, as well as having worked in state government and for the U.S. Department of Commerce. He offers sound advice for future communications executives, noting that those aspiring to head communications teams should first master "career building blocks": basic communication and interpersonal skills, and international exposure or experience.

Margaritis, whom I first met at a World Economic Forum in Davos, and got to know late in our careers, also encourages having a basic understanding of the legislative and regulatory processes that impact companies, thinking long-term and strategically, and building "business acumen." In a speech entitled "Lessons Learned in Building a Successful Career," he advised, "Be in a position to actively influence events and have the level of credibility among the business hierarchy; this includes knowledge of management, finance, marketing, and corporate strategy."

The CCO Gets a Makeover

I wholeheartedly agree that chief communicators need to be business executives, too. In former days, PR departments were rarely considered strategic assets and were often relegated to obscure floors. But like CEOs, many chief communicators today have MBAs and other advanced degrees. They have gained experiential business acumen and worldviews by working for global management consulting firms or holding line positions themselves. While leaders acknowledge that their chief communications officers are the experts when it comes to communication, it does not mean they will cut them slack in terms of understanding the company's business or that of its industry.

That is why the best communication executives are men and women who are all about substance. They study their companies and absorb as much critical information from external and internal sources as they can handle.

Dave Samson, general manager of public affairs at Chevron, said as much in a *PRWeek* article about the Arthur W. Page Society's "The New CCO" report. In it he described the forces transforming enterprises, both now and in the future, which will result in chief communications officers assuming a far more important and strategic role. "More than ever, the successful CCO is a leader in the enterprise, relied upon for their expertise in business, political, social, and cultural understanding, every bit as much as for their communications and stakeholder engagement expertise."

Elise Eberwein, the CCO for American Airlines, explained in *Chief Executive* magazine why CCOs are pivotal to CEOs, including new ones. A veteran of the airline industry who worked for CEO Doug Parker at America West and then at American Airlines after it merged with America West, Eberwein wrote that CCOs can have a highly valuable and productive partnership with their CEOs, especially following a transition. How?

"In the common occurrence of a CEO transition," she wrote, "it makes sense that the CCO would play a vital role in ensuring the transition is smooth, stakeholders are kept up to speed and that the new CEO's vision aligns with the internal corporate culture. To put it simply, the CCO is charged with protecting the reputation and legacy of the outgoing CEO, while ensuring acceptance of the new one. For this reason, they often best understand the benefits and pitfalls that may arise from the leadership change."

Eberwein said that type of high-level change management entails navigating internal politics, aligning the new CEO's vision and the company's culture, and "ensuring that values and vision for the company are not only communicated, but also are activated through clear policies and actions."

Communications executives will earn seats at the leadership table by capitalizing on their unique access to the three I's: information, intelligence, and insights. Organizations are awash in oceanic amounts of data. But individuals have to make sense of all that data—judging the potential opportunities and risks hidden in all the numbers and qualitative information.

It behooves communications chiefs to develop strong working relationships with the data analytics pros. They play a vital strategic role in interpreting trend lines, while also providing advantageous insights to the business units and their sales teams, who are always seeking an edge in the marketplace.

According to Abhinav Kumar, the chief communications and marketing officer for Tata Consultancy Services in Europe, "If communications departments can reinvent themselves to become 'intelligence centers,' the value of information that they can provide to the executive suite and boardrooms is absolutely unprecedented."

Kumar made that observation during a *PRWeek*-sponsored panel discussion. He also said that intelligence processing "has come to represent the largest opportunity ever for the communications profession. Through advanced listening tools and engagement, communicators have been put in an unprecedented position to capture the real-time pulse of any company's most crucial stakeholders—clients, influencers, employees, and even investors."

Kumar is right. He is also in the vanguard of a trend: chief communications and marketing positions are increasingly being consolidated into a single executive role.

Dozens of companies have already gone that route, forcing the collaboration of marketing and communications departments in working for the common good of the organization. Of course, this also gives an individual leader tremendous responsibility. When you are charged with leading both marketing and communications, you become the point person for both brand and institutional reputation.

This makes sense on many levels, just as it makes sense to have corporate security staff and cybersecurity personnel work together to protect the enterprise from sophisticated criminals and disruptors.

Kumar's observations about turning communication functions into intelligence centers are similar to those expressed by Dave Samson of Chevron. In an opinion piece that appeared in *PRWeek,* Samson wrote that communication chiefs should be builders "of digital engagement systems. With the bounty of data about stakeholders available to enterprises—everything from their relationships, actions, interests, physical locations, and so on—CCOs will develop highly personalized engagement through sophisticated data-driven systems. This is the beginning of an era where the comms function uses what it knows about stakeholders to develop a deeper understanding of their interests and needs and foster a deeper relationship with them. As the stakeholder universe becomes increasingly global, enterprises will need automated processes to engage the masses—not just as segments, but as individuals."

Follow the Clues

When mining for insights, millions of clues are available daily in posts, tweets, vlogs, blogs, and academic research—even the snark buzzing through affinity communities conversing on their favorite social media channels. But the trick is to have specialists hunting for those clues every day, acting as human weather vanes pointing in the direction changing winds are blowing. Because by the time behavioral patterns clustering on social media become teaser headlines on websites (e.g., "Marijuana Is the Next Craft Beer"), it's probably too late for an individual enterprise to capitalize as a first adopter.

The CCO needs to master modern media, employee engagement, research, public affairs, and other key disciplines. But the complete communications leader knows how his company operates, how it achieves profit margins, how it operates in foreign countries and cultures, how it creates and customizes products and solutions for its customers, and how its competitive advantages—if it has any—differentiate it from competitors in the marketplace.

In addition, a CCO must understand corporate governance, financial metrics and public disclosure regulations, cash flow and balance sheets, GAAP reporting and other accounting terminology and rules, and intellectual property. This is particularly important today with so many corporate leaders rising through finance and the CFO positions.

A communications chief with a talent for building cross-functional relationships can help enable collaborative leadership. Collaboration is what allows leadership teams to break down the silos that often create dysfunction and disharmony in organizations of all sizes, especially big ones.

Some organizations and employers are very specific about what they seek in chief communications executives. Here is an example from Kaiser Permanente, a company in Oakland, California. In its job description for a senior vice president–CCO, Kaiser advertised that it was looking for someone to handle essential responsibilities, including:

- Provide expert advice and counsel to the chairman and CEO and senior leadership, related to all aspects of communications.
- Develop KP's brand and reputation management strategy.
- Tell powerful stories, using technology effectively and reaching target audiences in impactful and engaging ways that are responsive to their needs and interests.
- Lead and manage an effective program-wide issues-management function that anticipates (when possible) and effectively responds to issues and events that pose a threat to the organization's reputation and performance.
- Collaborate with the CIO, SVP HR, SVP marketing, EVP health plan operations, and others to maintain

and enhance digital, social media, and other technologies and activities that support communication.

In addition, the job description listed more than a dozen expectations in terms of expertise and experience including:

- Successful experience working directly with board members and senior executives.
- Work experience within industries subject to intense regulatory and media scrutiny.
- Able to make strategic and succinct presentations to senior leadership.
- Successful experience as an organizational spokesperson in high-risk, high-visibility situations.

Kaiser also wanted a "strategic thinker, inspiring leader, effective manager, and team player who demonstrates credibility, integrity, and trust and is passionate about communications, with a can-do attitude about maintaining a market/industry leadership position for KP."

Wow. Finding those exact executive qualifications and mastery of communication expertise in one individual is a tall order, but credit Kaiser for listing all the desired qualities in its job search description.

A Matter of Respect

In a 2016 survey, Korn Ferry reported that two-thirds of respondents from Fortune 500 companies stated that the most important leadership characteristic for CCOs was a strategic mind-set with the ability to anticipate "future possibilities and [translate] them into breakthrough strategies."

In addition to having a strong communications leader, what else needs to be present in an organization's communication structure and ecosystem to make it most effective?

Like all members of a leader's executive team, the communications chief must be treated with respect. Even those who have served their companies well may be fired or marginalized when newly promoted chief executives, or new ones hired from the outside, appoint their own communications executives.

Because communication is so visible and has such an instantaneous effect, CCOs often experience blowback from other executives who think that news media coverage is something that can be entirely controlled. I have witnessed chief executives severely dressing down their communications chiefs in front of others. Some of these chewing-out tirades included profanity and belittling the person's value to the company. Other times, I have seen CCOs follow old agendas, putting them at odds with a new CEO with his own agenda.

I recall a CCO client who was having chemistry issues with a CEO recruited from outside the company to conduct a turnaround. The new CEO was known for occasional flare-ups with subordinates. But his displays of temper were for the most part theatrical, calculated to motivate those tasked with driving the company's turnaround.

I realized in this situation that the chief communications officer was not going to keep his position for long—not under the watch of a restless, results-driven leader who had apparently lost confidence in him. The new CEO was a big believer in strong communication networks connecting the company's customers, manufacturing facilities, employees, and vendors. I knew that to keep his company as a client, we had to help the CEO with his agenda.

I met with him privately to better understand his top priorities and sense of urgency. The conversation was friendly but direct. The company's performance turnaround was clearly job one, with plenty of need for strong communication around actions and initiatives the company would take. But one of his most vexing problems was external: an activist group targeting the company for alleged racial and age discrimination in its management practices. The company maintained the class action lawsuits filed by the group were without merit.

The activist group picketed the headquarters office and protested at the company's annual meeting. The new CEO believed that the company's approach to dealing with this situation—the lawsuits, the activist group's demands, and the impact on the company's reputation—was inadequate. He wanted fresh thinking. In our private meeting, he asked me what I thought he should do.

I organized a meeting of the best minds—from within his company and my firm—and did a situational analysis in order to recommend actions. At the meeting's conclusion, we walked the CEO through our learnings and recommendations. He listened attentively and asked that a plan be on his desk in a few days. What happened that day demonstrated what problem-solving teams must do to gain the confidence of a leader with a bias toward immediate action. The plan we came up with worked, the issue hanging over the company receded, and the CEO was better able to focus on his turnaround plan.

When there is a problem or situation that keeps a leader up at night, someone needs to take the lead and provide bold action. It can be a perfect opportunity for any executive, including the communications chief, to show off problem-solving skills, judgment, and toughness under pressure. I believe that in many situations, especially those with public implications like the one described on the previous pages, that leader can be—perhaps should be—the lead communications executive.

Why? As veteran communications chief Tony Cervone of General Motors once said, "Communications people must represent the outside world inside their companies." Cervone is not only good at doing just that, but he has also put into place the best systems and resources for monitoring the complex world in which a global enterprise like General Motors must operate.

Some public relations and communication pundits have categorically accused corporate leaders of being out of touch with societal change agents, corporate activists, and other antagonists. We acknowledge that a CEO is a mere mortal, neither a superhero nor a modern-day Nostradamus capable of seeing into the future. Which is why CEOs need to have people around them who can see opportunity and risk, trends and future consequences, and can thereby help the leader—and maybe the board of directors, too—to make the best decisions possible based on the best information available.

In a survey with leaders done by the Arthur Page Society, one CEO said that his chief communications officer was appointed to both his strategy and operating committees. "I'm expecting more than just the communications bit—I'm kind of expecting (the CCO to be) my right arm."

Go With Your Gut

I have sometimes advised clients based on experience and intuition rather than hard information. In one case, a CEO called my client, the chief communications officer, and me late the night before we were to execute a carefully organized, moment-by-moment communications plan. We were in her office working through the final details and contingency plans for an announcement about the divestiture of a major part of the company's operations.

The CEO was upset, having just learned that a reporter for the *Wall Street Journal*—one he particularly disliked and distrusted—had caught wind of the announcement and was calling company executives to confirm the impending announcement. The CEO understood that the reporter, who was well-known for news scoops, could upstage weeks of planning if an inaccurate, incomplete story were to be published the next morning.

"Let's put out our press release right now," ordered the CEO via speakerphone.

I took a deep breath and told the CEO that the reporter might not have enough information to sell it to his editor before the paper needed to go to press (this was before online editions). I also said there was a risk he might have the story, but that our carefully calibrated communications plan compelled us to take that risk and prepare to mobilize even earlier the next morning if a story did indeed appear.

After a long silence—and just before he hung up—the CEO said, "You better be right!"

I didn't sleep much that night. At about four-thirty the next morning, copies of the *Wall Street Journal* were delivered to the hotel lobby. I quickly went through the entire paper. No story.

The announcement went as planned. Later that morning I met with the CEO, who acknowledged that in the end my instincts had been correct. "But I would have kicked your butt out of here if you hadn't been right!" he admonished.

That's the kind of backhanded praise communication executives and their outside counselors sometimes receive from leaders—even when we are right. It comes with the territory.

"One thing's for sure," said *PRWeek*'s Barrett, "while PR pros don't operate under the same duress as firefighters, servicemen and women, or brain surgeons, they certainly exist in a highly charged and stressful environment that calls for experience, a cool head, and sage counsel under fire—all qualities these PR pros have in abundance."

A Slick Presentation Is Never Enough

Occasionally you meet a chief executive who has very good instincts about corporate reputation and its long-term value as a corporate asset. I first met and got to know Ed Whitacre in 2002, when he was traveling in Europe and gave a speech in Spain. He was the CEO of SBC Communications (later "renamed" AT&T after SBC acquired both the remaining businesses of AT&T and its brand identity).

At the time I was based in London, in my third year of managing FleishmanHillard's Europe, Middle East, and Africa operations. On another Whitacre trip to Europe in 2006, I was asked to accompany him for part of his business itinerary. In London between meetings, he asked if we could keep lunch simple and go to a pub for fish and chips. During lunch, he stepped away and found a quiet corner of the pub to take a call on his mobile phone. We realized several days later that the call was related to him closing another deal—the biggest in the company's history at the time. AT&T announced it was buying BellSouth, then the second largest of the Baby Bells, for $65 billion.

The year before, Whitacre had orchestrated one of the biggest deals in the industry when he acquired a faltering AT&T and integrated its impressive global enterprise businesses and technology prowess into SBC. As part of the BellSouth transaction, SBC would also acquire the remainder of the Cingular wireless company that it shared with BellSouth.

These back-to-back deals meant that Whitacre's team had doubled the size of SBC. In fact, given his previous acquisitions of Pacific Bell and Ameritech, Whitacre was in the process of reunifying a big part of the original pre-breakup AT&T. The company was able by late 2006 to win approval of the BellSouth deal in the United States and other countries that required government approval.

But while that was going on, Whitacre took a strong interest in what to call this massive new organization, which needed to meet the needs of millions of consumer customers across America and large business and institutional customers all over the world.

He was particularly concerned about what brand name would appeal to younger wireless customers, as well as about understanding what they were looking for from a mobile device and internet service provider. John Graham, FleishmanHillard's CEO at the time, had a strong relationship with Whitacre. He had also introduced to the company a number of excellent communication professionals, a few of whom, like Larry Solomon and

Selim Bingol, went on to be chief communication officers at the company.

Graham asked how we could help Whitacre in his decision-making process. We proposed doing a comprehensive brand research study; its findings could inform whatever corporate branding decision Whitacre eventually would make. Whitacre agreed, adding that he wanted the study done quietly and quickly.

I led the project and discreetly engaged a few of my colleagues and a few of SBC's marketing and research people to help. We had a hunch that Whitacre really liked the AT&T name as both a corporate and a consumer brand. We also believed that although he was leaning in that direction, he would be open-minded if the research suggested otherwise.

After doing primary and secondary research, we prepared our analysis and were ready to make recommendations. Graham and I met with Whitacre in his conference room and started walking him through a presentation summary. Long before this meeting, I had established trust and credibility with Whitacre, although I had yet to put it on the line in a high-stakes presentation.

Whitacre riffled through the first several pages of our summary, looking intently at each page but not commenting. After a while, he looked up over the glasses perched on his nose and glanced down to the far end of the long conference table, where we had lined up six thick binders, each stuffed with research data and summaries.

"Jack, is there anything in those binders?" Whitacre asked in his soft southwestern Texas drawl.

"Yes, all of our research is in those binders," I replied, surprised. "Do you want to see one?"

"No, just checking," he said, as though he were a poker player wondering if I had really drawn an inside straight. Whitacre was not only incredibly wise, but he wasn't going to be fooled by slick presentations. In his two decades as a CEO, he had sat through hundreds of presentations.

The point of this story is that as a leader Whitacre was also the communication chief. He engaged in a critical, long-term decision about the brand and the future promises it would represent to customers and other stakeholders. Whitacre was a leader who liked to cut to the chase. He required careful preparation, especially for public speaking and media interviews, but was a quick study. He could convert complex information, data, and talking points into his own genuine style, expressed in simple language.

That made him an excellent choice when the U.S. government, after extending General Motors a bailout, chose him to lead GM back to financial stability and fiscal responsibility. In his book *American Turnaround*, Whitacre talks about his early impressions once he took the helm at GM in 2009. One of the things he changed was to get executives to get rid of long PowerPoint presentations. "Just tell me what you need," he told the GM executives.

Plain talk and concision matter in leadership communication. Imagine all the time saved if more leaders told their underlings to "just tell me what you need."

Key Insights and Observations

- Leaders who have become able communicators know it takes a highly competent team to maximize their reach and effectiveness.
- First-class communication requires first-class resources.
- Communications executives will earn seats at the leadership table by capitalizing on their unique access to the three I's—information, intelligence, and insights.
- Collaborative leadership is what allows leadership teams to break down the silos that often create dysfunction and disharmony in big organizations.
- CEOs don't want yes-men as their CCOs—they want individuals who can contradict them and sometimes say no.

"We were hoping that you could work from work today."

7

Shift Happens

"The thing that I'm learning that has surprised me the most is you have a window of relevance, and unless you reinvent yourself within that window of relevance, you die."

—Kevin Systrom, co-founder of Instagram

Even winning organizations can die a slow death if what they do becomes less relevant. That's why leaders must have their organizational antennae constantly tuned for changing circumstances.

Change can be triggered by activists, market forces, customers, communities, whistle-blowers, generational employee differences, and technology shifts. It can come quickly, gradually, or unpredictably. But change always comes, no matter its velocity. Leaders cannot escape it. They can only anticipate, plan for, and deal with it.

Change forces leaders to act and communicate according to the situation and circumstances. By providing context about decisions that have short-term consequences and long-term significance, you are managing future expectations.

That's why leaders need to be on top of their communication game when navigating constant change. And they need the best communications advice they can find to interpret, communicate, and lead others through organizational change. We may live in an era of artificial intelligence, nanotechnology, virtual reality, interstellar travel, autonomous driving, and quantum computing. Still, it is ultimately humans who create change and humans who must manage the consequences of it. And that requires frequent and customized communications to keep the focus on the human benefits more than the technical wizardry behind change.

Change that can't be predicted is the bane of all leaders and business communicators. Markets change. Circumstances change. Priorities shift within an organization. External events—so-called exogenous factors—happen. Continually. And while not much seems predictable in the twenty-first century, we depend on leaders for historical perspective and their forecasting abilities. We want them to use their wisdom to draw upon valuable lessons from the organization's past.

Many older companies have been through cycles of change—ups, downs, turnarounds, and transformations. AT&T and the Bell system. IBM. Breweries and distilleries that have been around for centuries. Automakers, insurers, and industrial concerns from Germany to Japan to the U.S. The leaders of companies and countries must possess the foresight to identify the positive signs of better times ahead even when the future seems bleak and doubtful.

Take the Long View

A good example is McDonald's, which has been an icon of success for most of its sixty-plus years in business. But the Chicago-based company has certainly experienced rough patches over the last two decades, during which seven CEOs have presided over a matrixed enterprise that is both a global corporation and a system of franchisees, which is what McDonald's calls its owner-operators. (Eighty percent of the company's more than thirty-seven thousand restaurants are operated by franchisees.)

Steve Easterbrook, McDonald's CEO since 2015, put that unique relationship into perspective in an interview with CNBC's Jim Cramer: "Our success is mutually dependent. So the company will never be successful without the owner-operators on board, and vice versa. What we had to do was instill some trust, some excitement, some confidence—confidence in our leadership, but also confidence that as they invest and commit themselves ... there is future growth and that there is future capital opportunities for them. That takes a lot of collaborating, and we invest a lot of time in that. But as momentum in the business grows, the confidence grows. As confidence grows, this sort of mojo returns."

For Easterbrook, it has been more of a transformation than a restoration. His comments show that he has a sense of the McDonald's history and how it has ridden the roller coaster of change as consumer preferences have evolved. He also offers fresh perspective as a former competitor. Unlike other past McDonald's chiefs, Easterbrook left the company in 2011 to take leadership positions at other casual-dining companies. He returned to McDonald's in 2013 and two years later became CEO at a time when the business was struggling. Performance improved under his leadership, and the company's stock price reached all-time highs. Easterbrook played cricket in England in his youth, and certain cricket matches can last for days before an outcome is certain. As a result, he seems to know instinctively how things can change.

By 2019, his team remained under pressure to boost sales performance in the U.S., its biggest market. But Easterbrook took the long view, believing the turnaround mission for McDonald's was not just to respond to changing times and consumer preferences. He wanted to get ahead of the curve and to do so with the complete and enthusiastic support of the McDonald's owner-operators.

"As a CEO you have three resources—people, financial, and time. The one thing competitors were doing better than us was time. We were slowly getting less relevant," said Easterbrook, who has said he admires how agile companies like Amazon and Uber have changed customer expectations on speed and service.

The drive-through, which accounts for 55 percent of all McDonald's traffic, is one such service, allowing people to stay in their cars and continue talking or texting. Service is experiential, however, and the convenience of a McDonald's drive-through only equates to a plus if orders are delivered promptly and correctly. As Howard Schultz, former chairman of Starbucks, once said, "Coffee is the product, but not the business we are in."

Earlier in my career, business, marketing, and investor communications were much simpler disciplines. Everything changed with the advent of the internet, digital media, and people's reliance on smart devices for everything from making lunch dates to choosing a new refrigerator to buy. As a result, communications have been forced into perpetual reinvention.

That's why I believe that leading change—as Easterbrook is doing at McDonald's—is hard work. Perhaps even endless work.

Kevin Systrom, Instagram's former CEO, told the *Wall Street Journal* in 2017 of his own experience, "I call it the 'success syndrome,' where you're successful, you do all the things that made you successful and you keep doing those things thinking that that's why you're going to be successful in the future. Things change."

Change Is a Full-Time Job

I gave a speech in 2016 on that very subject. Its title referenced a speech given by twentieth-century Illinois statesman Adlai Stevenson II, a governor and two-time Democratic presidential nominee, who said, "Change for the better is a full-time job." I would like to underscore the words *for the better*. What follows in this chapter are some of the observations I made in that speech.

Change can take leaders and their organizations in different directions. Good and bad. ***Change for the better*** **is what organizations strive for every day on behalf of stakeholders. But the obstacles and counterforces to achieving positive outcomes during periods of rapid change have never been more demanding.**

The digital evolution of new communication technologies has disrupted everything we do and how we do it. We have gone from an old world of news conferences and long-term campaigns to programmatic media buying, automated tweet distribution, drone-captured video materials, and *daily* multimedia brand-building campaigns. **Communications is the nerve system of change, stimulating all parts of organizations to work together while sensing pain points and systemic roadblocks.** The old ways of doing things and communicating about them now face limitations. Town hall meetings, webcasts, and the like still have their place, but rumors and information sources outside the organization circulated via fast channels also exert influence over sentiments and mind-sets.

Scott Galloway, NYU Stern School of Business professor, author, and acclaimed speaker on technology trends, said this about disruption and communications technology: "Probably not enough people in our business are true communications technology entrepreneurs, but we're going to see more of that in the future. We've seen it in the social media realm, where entrepreneurs can take the technology and apply it to everyday communication...It's not a matter of us coming up with a new product. We have to start thinking in ways beyond just adapting to the technology; it's a matter of trying to foresee what comes next and after that, how new communications technologies will be evolving."

Leaders trying to lead change and transformation programs face headwinds and obstacle courses. Let's look at just a few of the forces buffeting organizations and compelling constant reaction, rethinking, and recalibration.

Oh, the Pressure!

First, competition is coming at companies at every level and from all directions. Just when you think you have all bases covered, a new competitor pops up or a known one changes the game. It's enough to make even the best leaders feel like soldiers in a foxhole, dodging incoming fire while trying to focus on longer-range combatant targets. Global organizations work 24-7, meaning that every hour of every day, people are working across time zones and crossing oceans aboard airplanes. Yet it's hard enough trying to effect change in just one location, or even in one country.

It is especially difficult for multinational organizations, as language, culture, and operational differences add complexities to the job of communicating new directions. The velocity of change makes change seem continuous, with no endpoint, even if goals have been achieved. It reminds me of a Winston Smith line about war in George Orwell's *1984*: "The war is not meant to be won. It is meant to be continuous." Because when your organization is shifting and pivoting, so are your competitors. Or maybe other events are occurring, such as regulators enacting or reinforcing laws. Or consumer attitudes about specific products or services falling in trend-driven disfavor. Nothing stands still while leaders make strategic moves. It is always a multidimensional chess match in which you must anticipate countermoves by opponents.

Competing with Strong Ideas

Ian Schrager, the entrepreneur who gave us the world-renowned disco nightclub Studio 54 during the 1970s, went on to be a successful owner of trendy boutique hotels. Like cab companies disrupted by Uber and other ride-sharing services, the hotel business has been disrupted by the likes of Airbnb, which a Morgan Stanley study found has been used by at least a quarter of all travelers. "Airbnb is a mortal threat to the U.S. hotel industry," Schrager predicted in an article in the *Wall Street Journal*. "The only way you can compete with a strong idea is by having another strong idea."

In Schrager's case, the strong idea was the opening of Public, his luxury hotel on New York City's Lower East Side. What makes his concept different is that it offers lower room rates made possible by sophisticated self-check-in technology and limited services, which allows Public to employ fewer desk clerks and other traditional hotel workers. Whether the concept works against Airbnb remains to be seen.

Advertising and marketing comprise an industry that has been responding to rapid change for—well, for decades. Every new period of change in consumer behavior, research techniques, media consumption trends, and disruptive information technology has reshaped the advertising and marketing services agency world, which by some accounts is a $1 trillion industry. Few know this better than John Wren, the CEO of Omnicom Group for the past two decades. "The key topic that is keeping many of the world's top marketers up at night is how to manage disruption in their business, whether it's threats from new competitors or keeping pace with changing consumer behaviors," Wren told analysts and investors during a quarterly earnings call.

The Road to Change

Carmakers are among the biggest global marketers, spending billions annually on marketing. They also must continuously reinvent aspects of their businesses, everything from sales channels to power sources for the cars themselves. This story about Chrysler Corporation is an example of a leader and a company responding to marketplace change and criticism by taking command of the situation, even if the results of that campaign would not bear fruit until the new cars were ready to sell much later. But such are the challenges of those who manufacture industrial products and big-ticket items that cannot be modified as quickly as consumables.

I worked as a consultant to the Chrysler communications team at a time when the company and its legendary CEO Lee Iacocca were again confronting serious headwinds. Sales were lackluster and car industry pundits were criticizing the company for not being innovative and bringing new product designs to market.

One of my assignments for Chrysler was to draft message points for the company's year-end earnings release and press briefing. The Chrysler comms team sensed that Iacocca had become frustrated with the industry tradition at the time of providing sales data every ten days. No other industry then had been subjected to reporting its sales progress three times a month.

With that in mind, I wrote something to the effect that Chrysler was making big plans, including product innovations, for the next ten years, and that it should no longer be judged strictly on ten-day sales performance. Iacocca apparently liked that theme and used it in the briefing. But he also wanted to demonstrate in big ways to the company's admirers and detractors alike that Chrysler was an innovator and change maker in the industry. And he wanted it quickly. As Iacocca once said, "I've always found that the speed of the boss is the speed of the team."

Swinging into action, the marketing and communications executives at Chrysler reprised something they had done before: showcasing prototype, preproduction Chrysler cars on a multicity road trip. VIPs in strategic cities would get sneak previews of "Chrysler in the '90s" and the opportunity to talk with Iacocca and other Chrysler executives. Working closely with Chrysler's then communications chief Steve Harris and his team, we scheduled and staffed high-level media interviews with Iacocca and the other executives.

It was a PR success. But more importantly, the campaign bought valuable time for the company to finish a new platform of cars that would not be marketed for another eighteen months. Another Chrysler comeback like the one in the 1980s followed in the 1990s, with change again driven from the top.

Crisis as Change Agent

Few events compel organizational or industry change like a crisis. Crisis can overwhelm any company, not to mention the many other players caught in its wake. Financial crises force government regulators and policy makers to rethink conventional economic wisdom that no longer fits a global economy that behaves asymmetrically. Major data breaches cause intelligence and public service agencies to question their firewalls, protocols, and risk-management programs. Food and health crises shake the foundational beliefs of scientists and medical authorities. And the public.

It was Rahm Emanuel who said, "You never want a serious crisis to go to waste." That was 2008 and he was about to join the new Obama administration as the White House chief of staff. The U.S. and many other economies were suffering the effects of a Wall Street meltdown and the threat of a disastrous global economic recession. The context for Emanuel's point was the 1973–1974 energy crisis in America, which he said had been an opportunity to boldly rethink how to address the nation's long-term energy needs, and that in hindsight it was a crisis wasted. In short, he was suggesting that the 2008 banking crisis was an opportunity to reset long-term policies.

Organizations that attempt to merely survive a crisis are making a mistake. A crisis is the perfect time for recovery, discovery, and taking lessons learned into positive initiative.

It takes unusual leadership, strong character, and will to pivot from a crisis to something positive. In the middle of General Motors' massive ignition switch recall in 2014, new CEO Mary Barra saw the crisis as a platform for precipitating change at GM. As she told *Forbes* magazine, "We want to do the right thing and serve the customer well through this—but it is also an opportunity to accelerate cultural change." She has been doing that ever since in an effort to prove that General Motors can be the industry leader in this century that it was for most of the last century.

Activists at the Gate

I have had the good fortune of working with other industry leaders including McDonald's, AT&T, Monsanto, BP, Caterpillar, Baxter, KPMG, JPMorgan Chase, and Procter & Gamble. P&G has gone through multiple CEOs in just the past few decades. That included bringing back the highly respected A. G. Lafley for a second tour of duty after the board ousted his successor, Bob McDonald. Lafley was considered open-minded to outside thinking and flexible in trying—and perhaps failing—with new ideas. He is also remembered as a good listener. "Let's execute along this strategy, but know that we'll probably get some of this wrong, so be open to changing it," Lafley once said.

According to billionaire investor-activist Nelson Peltz, P&G has gotten much wrong in recent times, despite selling off a hundred of the brands it considered less strategic to the company's future. Peltz, chairman of the hedge fund Trian Partners, launched an activist campaign in 2017 to force major changes at P&G, a campaign that was opposed vehemently by P&G CEO David Taylor and his board of directors.

Peltz, who was also campaigning for a seat on P&G's board, took his proxy battle to the business media, both print and broadcast. He was regularly interviewed on CNBC, Fox News, and other programs.

Peltz recommended reorganizing P&G into three business lines. In one TV appearance, Peltz referred to watching "an iceberg melt"—a reference to his view that P&G was incapable of making rapid change in order to reverse its fortunes.

P&G spent a reported $65 million to stave off Peltz's incursion, the most expensive corporate election ever. Taylor, who was in his first year as the company's CEO, used leadership communication to reach out to his employees, shareholders, customers, and business and civic leaders in P&G's longtime headquarters city of Cincinnati. He acknowledged that shifting consumer habits would pose ongoing challenges to P&G's strategy of sustaining growth through innovation and improved products. As Taylor told one CNBC interviewer, "Ultimately it's about winning the consumer value equation; it's working with our customers and working very hard to create and build categories as the key driver of growth."

The reputation of a CEO—or any leader—is based on the collective perceptions of stakeholders across many categories of interest, concern, and investment. Perceptions are dynamic, not static. The perception was that Taylor should stay at P&G's helm. Peltz, who challenged the proxy vote by P&G shareholders, ultimately won a board seat after a recount.

Like Peltz, Carl Icahn has been an activist investor for decades. The Wall Street titan has earned such nicknames as "buyout master" and "corporate raider" as a result of his aggressive investment strategies.

Icahn's investment approach is to target companies he believes are undervalued and perhaps mismanaged, acquire a controlling interest in those companies, and then become the most important shareholder with the ability to leverage change—including new board of director appointees and business-performance turnaround plans. Now in his eighties, Icahn relies on Twitter and other social media to stay abreast of news about companies on his target list.

In late 2017 he targeted Xerox, which had been split into two companies a few months earlier. Why Xerox? "The CEO is the most important person in the company," Icahn told the *Wall Street Journal.* "We believe Xerox still has potential, but it will go the way of Kodak if there aren't major changes. Times have changed but not the old guard that controls the board."

Icahn and Peltz represent a category of corporate disrupters who often strike terror in the hearts of corporate leaders and board directors. Their intentions may seem noble in that they can magnify shareholder frustration and drive change in targeted companies. But their overall goal is to win no matter what. Either they gain control of the companies they target, or they use frenzied proxy fights to drive up stock prices and the value of the shares they control. On slow news days, they can attract a lot of attention and airtime, forcing their targets to either react to or ignore the media attacks. After they have satisfied their goals with one target, they move on to the next.

A different kind of activist investor is CEO Laurence Fink of BlackRock, who has taken a novel position on shareholder activism. BlackRock is the largest institutional fund manager in the world, with more than $6 trillion under management. In his 2018 annual letter to the CEOs of companies in which BlackRock invests, Fink espoused "a new model of shareholder engagement—one that strengthens and deepens communication between shareholders and the companies that they own." In past letters, Fink talked about companies focusing too much on quarterly results, and not enough about long-term value creation. "Similarly," he wrote, "shareholder engagement has been too focused on annual meetings and proxy votes."

Fink said in the letter and in media interviews that BlackRock would put that model into practice by doubling its staff dedicated to communications and relationships with the companies in its vast portfolio. In addition to having conversations with those companies about their financial performance and long-term strategies, he indicated that BlackRock would also be assessing how those companies are responding to changing business, social, and public policy trends.

"A central reason for the rise of activism—and wasteful proxy fights—is that companies have not been explicit enough about their long-term strategies," Fink told CNBC anchors in an interview at the World Economic Forum.

Paul Polman, the former CEO of Unilever, had a different take on the rise of hostile activism. He expressed it in an interview with the *Financial Times* after Kraft Heinz made a hostile bid for his company in 2017. Polman believed that quantitative easing by central banks had placed too much available capital in circulation for potential corporate takeovers. And he suggested the rise of passive shareholder investment made board takeover attempts less challenging. So he was not surprised that so many global companies were being pursued by activist shareholders. "If you (a company) don't have an activist, you feel like you're doing something wrong these days," he said.

Activism is commonly used to oppose or change corporate policies, leadership, governance, cultural behavior, or structure. The tools to express activism and coalesce public support are familiar to communications professionals: rallies, protests, public petitions, tweets and other social media commentary, litigation, and talk show call-ins.

Today we are seeing heightened activism both directed at institutions and advocated by the institutions themselves. Companies become activists in hostile takeovers. Hedge funds and aggressive investors target vulnerable companies.

Companies employ sophisticated defenses to fight off raiders and other antagonists.

Threats from Within

Whistle-blowers and citizen journalists are also keeping organizations on guard. Any public event or private moment can be captured on a smartphone and shared with the world—with or without the help of news organizations. For instance, in 2017 an Indiana elementary school district was embarrassed when a student peeked through the window of a locked classroom door, saw a teacher snorting cocaine, and recorded her on his smartphone. The video went viral and the school district had to scramble, moving quickly to suspend the teacher, who was eventually charged.

Communication flows ever faster, but human decision making hasn't kept pace with the technology behind it. When someone asks, "Why did that executive team take so long to respond to the situation?" it's because that team is made up of human beings, who process things at a more deliberate rate than the speed of communications allows.

The increasing speed of communications underscores the imperative of having people in the communications profession who are skilled at public relations and public affairs, and who are always at the ready to deal with situations that require immediate attention. In a world where things happen quickly, there has to be someone capable of running interference between a controversial issue and a leader.

In addition to outside threats, the leader must contend with the complexity of his own workforce. Today it is not inconceivable to have multiple generations of employees working together, from workers in their teens to those in their mid-seventies, a reality Hollywood captured in *The Intern*, a film starring Robert De Niro and Anne Hathaway.

As a result, leaders must be sensitive to generational differences and communicate effectively to each segment. At the same time, they also must understand what connects individual employees of all ages, genders, and demographic differences.

Sometimes it seems as though big organizations care about wasting time, money, or energy, but are unconcerned about wasting human potential. Leaders need to regard the potential of the collective brainpower and willpower of all those around them. Too few organizations *crowdsource* and incentivize enough good ideas from their own people. No wonder so many workers feel their capacities are underutilized. In a 2017 Korn Ferry survey of nearly five thousand professionals, a third of the respondents said their jobs were boring and they needed new challenges. That was the top reason for leaving a company, ahead of the 24 percent who cited a poor cultural fit as the impetus for quitting their jobs.

Leadership communication can be a motivator for encouraging employees to succeed in the face of great challenges. Businesses generally strive to be better servants to their customers. But to perform better for customers and end users, businesses first need the collective commitment of their people. Without that, change for the better is improbable and more likely impossible. And there we enter the realm of human performance psychology. What motivates people? What do our workplace colleagues really want? Here are the most common employee needs, all of which require and depend on clear leadership communication:

- Employees need a sense of shared purpose to find passion and meaning in their work.
- People want clear direction about the end goals of the company and the performance measures on which they collectively will be judged.
- Workers expect to be judged on shorter-term metrics but want the long-term context, too, especially about their contributions to the greater good.
- If the company grows, employees expect to achieve personal growth and career ascension, particularly if their performances warrant it.
- Money—competitive pay and benefits—matters.

Recognizing how the generational needs of employees differ is also a challenge. Millennials already exercise power over social mores and values, public thought, product design, style and fashion, payment choices, and a host of other things. In the workplace, millennials want to fulfill their talents completely. They seek mentoring. They want to have time to pursue personal innovation, development, or community service. They want *immersive* learning experiences. And many of them do not want to be typecast as millennials.

Gen Xers want some of those courtesies, too, as well as promotions and the opportunity for upward mobility, skills retraining, and a voice in company direction and policy. Baby boomers want to conclude their careers as successfully as possible. They seek professional reinvention and coaching to allay retirement anxieties.

Each generation is now participating and competing in the so-called *gig economy* as independent contractors. They are mobile, independent, and less loyal, which represents yet another management challenge. Demographic trends suggest that independent contractors with desirable skills will result in a seller's market wherever and whenever the demand for skilled workers is high.

Once again, leaders need to have skilled communication professionals at their sides to speak to different generations in language that's most relevant to their situations. This allows leaders to communicate more authentically. And we expect our leaders to be authentic, according to FleishmanHillard's annual study entitled "The Authenticity Gap." Here are a few key insights according to the 2018 study:

- Authentic CEOs must be open and honest about why they are taking a stand on social matters. Ninety percent of the consumers surveyed said they perceived that companies sometimes or often wade into social issues primarily for their own benefit.

- Our expectations for management to do the right thing are on the rise. The authentic CEO must be visible in the right ways. As the FH study revealed, what the CEO says and does is critical to the way a company is perceived. More than three-quarters (78 percent) of those questioned strongly agreed that the behaviors and integrity of the CEO reflected the behaviors and integrity of the company he or she leads.

Another leadership challenge: the ever-shifting attitudes around information and privacy. For every good intention and action to keep employees well informed, there also lurks the threat posed by hackers and data thieves, who take advantage of doors left open by human error or poorly regulated internal information-security controls. Indeed, this vulnerability has shown up in the practical and ideological struggle between companies like Apple and the government—a battle of privacy versus national and community security that prompted Apple CEO Tim Cook to declare "privacy as a fundamental right."

Yet the conundrum is this: the more information organizations collect and share with their employees, customers, and business partners, the more vulnerable private or privileged information becomes. And that's because e-commerce and e-communications are now a way of life.

Politics, sports, and celebrity and pop culture have accelerated the evolution of social media more than ever. We are no longer content as consumers of news and information; we want to be part of the story. We want to be commentators tweeting or blogging about it. We want to be in the picture—literally. Presidential candidates, prime ministers, athletes, and celebrities of all kinds now are obligated to pose for countless selfies whenever they engage their publics in person. Even popes and religious leaders participate actively in the Twitter, Instagram, and Facebook world. And the breathless pace of political campaigns has demonstrated how rapidly messages and even policy positions are adjusted to seize opportunity and quell threats.

Making Change Work

Leader-communicators have the potential to be difference makers in our world, even if the process can be scary. You can be an architect of a plan or program to lead change. In fact, you may be working right now in partnership with leading management consulting firms, like McKinsey, Booz Allen Hamilton, or BCG on a program aimed at changing the organization from its present state to how you wish it to be positioned and to perform in the future.

Companies such as Apple, Marvel, Netflix, Delta Airlines, Burberry, Lego, Fiat Chrysler, and Converse, to name a few, have experienced remarkable turnarounds in their existences.

But how do you make positive change sustainable?

First, a leader needs to examine the enterprise's strengths and weaknesses and determine the necessary structural changes that will best enable the change. The next step is to define a unifying purpose and create with organizational leaders—and with representative employee input—the new goals and strategies of the change campaign. All of this has to work not only within the current culture but also with foresight about the cultural changes sought.

In addition, the plan needs many leaders to drive it. They may not necessarily be functional or business-unit leaders but can be others chosen for their unique skills to shape, communicate, and implement the plan. Mind-set and actual behavior changes that impact performance are key metrics. Pressure testing the plan in smaller groups is also advisable before rolling it out across the organization. Key performance metrics will define success and accountability. Internal enthusiasm for the change program and a positive customer experience resulting from it are key indicators of success.

When trying to redirect an organization that has drifted from its purpose, leadership communication—and leadership by example—should be frequent, interactive, and personified by compelling stories of progress. Rewards and promotions must be aligned to financial and operational performance. They must also encourage the most desirable cultural behaviors. To quote a CEO from the digital commercial printing and logistics industry with whom I once worked closely on his organization's change campaign, the most important six words in a transformational change campaign are "follow up, follow up, follow up."

When change comes in the form of a leadership transition, the new leader has to often set a different course while honoring the work and legacy of an organization's founder. That was clearly the case of Satya Nadella replacing Steve Ballmer as CEO of Microsoft, while staying true to the mission of Bill Gates.

Writing about Microsoft in the *Harvard Business Review,* Michael Schrage noted that "Microsoft's ongoing global challenge isn't how well the CEO articulates a compelling innovation vision but how creatively its legions of sales teams, marketers, project managers, and coders translate those ideas into persuasive actions. The company requires a new vocabulary to express its increasingly innovative self. ...Entrepreneurial founders, of course, have both semantic and rhetorical advantages over their successors in this regard. A company's creator disproportionately owns and influences its vocabulary. But every CEO leading change and confronting disruption needs people and systems in place that assure key words are understood by all."

Let There Be Light

Change can be forced upon organizations—even great, old sports franchises.

What follows is an example of change driven by competitors and new ownership despite challenges posed by tradition and community resistance.

The current owners of the Chicago Cubs, the Ricketts family, hired turnaround wizard Theo Epstein, manager Joe Maddon, and others of great talent to turn perennial losers into the 2016 World Series champions. But long before the Ricketts family bought the team, something else had to happen to lay the groundwork for future success. That something else was night baseball.

In 1981, ownership of the Cubs shifted from the Wrigley family to the Chicago-based Tribune Company. At that time, the Cubs were the only team in Major League Baseball not to have a stadium equipped with lights for night baseball. By the 1950s, most established MLB teams had lighted facilities. In the decades to follow, frustrated National League team owners came to resent losing a percentage of Wrigley Field ticket sales because they were unable to take advantage of higher attendance for night games.

The Tribune Company in the 1980s was determined to either get night baseball or look elsewhere to build a new, lighted stadium. The obstacles to remaining at Wrigley Field, however, were numerous. One was a community group called Citizens United for Baseball Sunshine (CUBS). CUBS represented residents of the North Side neighborhood surrounding Wrigley Field who opposed night baseball due to fears about noise, congestion, parking problems, excessive drinking, and vandalism.

With its "No Lights" signs and T-shirts pervasively on display throughout Wrigleyville, as the neighborhood was known, CUBS was an extremely effective opponent. There was political opposition as well. The governor, the Illinois General Assembly, the mayor of Chicago, and the local Chicago alderman representing the ward in which Wrigleyville resided all opposed lights.

But by 1987, the Cubs were coming up on the eightieth anniversary of their *last* World Series championship, and forty-two years since they had played in a World Series. Polls indicated that most Cubs fans in metropolitan Chicago favored some night baseball at Wrigley, even if the Wrigleyville community did not.

In 1987 I was doing work for the Tribune Company, which at the time owned the *Chicago Tribune*, many other metro newspapers, and broadcast properties such as WGN television and radio. And the Cubs. My Tribune client Joseph "Andy" Hays arranged for me to meet with Don Grenesko, the executive VP of the Cubs organization. Grenesko and I discussed how to get local government approval to install lights at Wrigley Field, lights that were essential to the Cubs' future. But the Tribune Company for several years had lobbied local politicians to repeal laws prohibiting night baseball at Wrigley Field, and went to court several times in the pursuit of night baseball.

Grenesko wanted a game plan for success. I was curious to know when the neighborhood's residents had last been surveyed on whether they still opposed the lights proposition. I suggested a new poll, but as it turned out we didn't need one. The city's Economic Development Commission was conducting a poll on its own. What was even better was that the new poll came back positive thanks to new night-game conditions agreed to by the Cubs and the city.

In the end, 59 percent of those polled in Wrigleyville said they would support—or at least not block—night baseball if the Cubs enforced four conditions, two of which called on the team to limit night play to eighteen home games (out of eighty-one) and halt the sale of alcohol after the seventh inning.

Whether it was the favorable survey results or fear surrounding the fact that the Tribune Company seemed serious about moving the team to a Chicago suburb, city hall changed its thinking about night baseball at Wrigley Field.

After the baseball season ended in 1987, Chicago mayor Harold Washington worked out a deal between the city and the Cubs. And although Washington died two weeks later of a heart attack, the City Council approved limited night baseball at Wrigley.

In this case, the new research on what would move the community and politicians to accept night baseball at Wrigley was crucial. That and some patience to allow political forces to play out as the Tribune's choice became clearer: lights at Wrigley Field or a new lighted stadium outside the city.

Fast-forward to today. Wrigley Field looks the same in many ways—famous for its brick walls, ivy-covered outfield perimeter, and ancient and iconic centerfield scoreboard. What's new are Jumbotrons, digital messaging and advertising, elevators, faster in-park mobile service, a stadium-side park, a hotel and commercial development, Pearl Jam and Billy Joel concerts on open dates, and more of the spectacular features common to modern-day stadiums.

But in 2019 the Ricketts family faced their first true embarrassing controversy as Cubs owner. *Splinter,* a news and opinion site owned by Univision, disclosed anti-Islamic emails sent by Joe Ricketts, the family's seventy-seven-year old patriarch and self-made billionaire. Ricketts's son Tom Ricketts joined his father in apologizing for the bigoted screeds, but he also took further remedial action. The Cubs chairman met with the leaders of several local Muslim organizations and agreed to have notable Muslims participate in Cubs and Wrigley Field traditions, anti-hate PSAs featuring Cubs personnel, and Cubs support for other community initiatives.

"We are encouraged the Cubs, led by Tom Ricketts, responded swiftly and genuinely in partnering with us to turn the situation around," said Ahmed Rehab, Chicago chapter executive director of the Council on American-Islamic Relations. "As a result, the Cubs are taking a significant step forward and will use the power of their brand and voice to fight Islamophobia, racism, and bigotry."

As for that first night game at Wrigley Field in 1988, Grenesko asked me for ideas about engaging the community for the advent of night baseball at Wrigley. During one of our meetings in 1988, he showed me three potential dates for the first night game and asked my opinion. One of the proposed dates was August 8—8-8-88. It was the obvious choice.

Of course, in keeping with the Cubs' bad luck, that first night game at Wrigley was rained out in the fourth inning.

Key Insights and Observations

- Change and disruption forces leaders to take the offensive in both their actions and communications.
- Communications is the nerve system of change, stimulating all parts of organizations to work together while sensing pain points and systemic roadblocks.
- Leadership communication can be a motivator for encouraging employees to succeed in the face of great challenges.
- Communication flows ever faster, but human decision making hasn't kept pace with the technology behind it.
- When trying to redirect an organization that has drifted from its purpose, leadership communication—and leadership by example—should be frequent, interactive, and personified by compelling stories of progress.
- Managing and inspiring employees ranging across four generations is another challenge today's leaders must meet.
- Activism is clearly a forceful instrument of change. We will likely see more activism directed at institutions as well as some advocated and energized by the institutions themselves.

"You can't legislate morality, thank heaven."

8

Stand Up for Change

"It is a leader's role, in business or in government, to bring people together, not tear them apart."

—Jamie Dimon, Chairman, JPMorgan Chase

In past years, people marched in the streets for equality, social justice, and better working conditions. Today they march for—and sometimes against—a wide swath of issues: Living wages instead of minimum wages. Transgender washrooms. Gender pay equality. Ethical treatment of the aged. Ethical treatment of animals. Climate change. Confederate flags. Gun control. Black Lives Matter. Campus rape and assault. Immigration reform. Abortion rights. Police brutality.

And that's just in America.

We are living in a new era in which corporate leaders have joined the stewards of NGOs and social activists in challenging public positions on government policies that affect their employees, customers, stakeholders, and society in general. Concerns range from the commercial to the humanitarian.

Larry Fink, CEO of BlackRock, told fellow CEOs in his 2019 "Purpose and Profits" letter that the "world needs your leadership."

"Unnerved by fundamental economic changes and the failure of government to provide lasting solutions," Fink said, "society is increasingly looking to companies, both public and private, to address pressing social and economic issues." Fink even suggested companies have an obligation to do so.

"As divisions continue to deepen, companies must demonstrate their commitment to the countries, regions, and communities where they operate, particularly on issues central to the world's future prosperity," Fink said. "Companies cannot solve every issue of public importance, but there are many—from retirement to infrastructure to preparing workers for the jobs of the future—that cannot be solved without corporate leadership."

Jamie Dimon's words cited at the beginning of this chapter came in the heated days following the violent events of Charlottesville, Virginia, in 2017. That's when white nationalists, outraged by the city's plan to remove a statue of Confederate general Robert E. Lee, organized a rally. The tiki torch–carrying marchers were confronted by counter-protesters, a clash that resulted in rioting and the death of a young woman.

In the wake of the violence and ensuing controversial statements made by President Trump, Dimon wrote a memo, distributed throughout JPMorgan Chase, that echoed the comments of other CEOs who had resigned from the president's advisory councils on business policy and job-creating initiatives: "Racism, intolerance, and violence are always wrong."

Not long after Charlottesville, Dimon spoke on a quarterly earnings conference call. In the words of the *Wall Street*

Journal, he "let loose with a high-quality harangue against the political class." According to a transcript of the call, Dimon had this to say: "Since the Great Recession, which is now eight years old, we've been growing at 1.5 percent to 2 percent in spite of stupidity and political gridlock...We are unable to build bridges, we're unable to build airports, our inner-city schoolkids are not graduating."

In addition to running one of the six largest banks in the world, Dimon is chairman of the Business Roundtable and is involved in other civic and business organizations. During a question-and-answer session with more than three hundred members of the Economic Club of Chicago, he enumerated problems that "need to be fixed" in America: the disparity in education opportunities, lending to small businesses, declining wages, globally uncompetitive U.S. corporate tax policy, affordable housing, and other societal issues.

Dimon said that his first responsibility is to make JPMorgan Chase financially successful: "Without that nothing else matters." But his outspokenness on issues is reminiscent of something Eleanor Roosevelt once said: "Do what you feel in your heart. For you'll be criticized anyway." Nonetheless, many leaders prefer to steer clear of criticism of themselves and the organizations they lead. To wit, Robert Eccles, Scott Newquist, and Roland Schatz wrote a decade ago in the *Harvard Business Review* that "senior executives tend to be optimists and cheerleaders. Their natural inclination is to believe the praise heaped on their companies and to discount criticism."

After the Charlottesville outrage from the public and some CEOs, *Wall Street Journal* columnist Holman W. Jenkins Jr. noted that "Companies get in bed with politicians when it serves their interests and are quick to run away when it doesn't. Thus nobody is obliged to interpret the flutter of CEOs away from President Trump's advisory council since the Charlottesville riot as occasion of courage."

It takes courage for business leaders to speak out against government or social policies. Many do. We focus on them in this chapter. But those that do must calculate the risk-reward of staking out opinions that may not be in sync with all of their many corporate stakeholders.

I remember the days when CEOs preferred to avoid the proverbial third rail of sensitive public issues, primarily out of fear of alienating customers, shareholders, and other key constituencies. Dimon, however, is representative of a growing number of outspoken corporate leaders no longer willing to be reticent about societal issues and the government policy failures that make headlines. Dimon is also a leader willing to accept responsibility, sometimes begrudgingly, for his institution's occasional mistakes—mistakes like the "London Whale" derivatives trading loss of $6.2 billion that highlighted a systemic risk management failure at the bank.

Biggest Business on Earth

For two and half centuries, the U.S. government at all levels has created as many agencies, laws, regulations, and commissions as the taxpaying citizenry is willing to tolerate. As Calvin Coolidge famously said, "The business of government is business." Government today is one of the biggest businesses on

Earth—biggest employer, biggest user of the planet's resources, biggest fiduciary of pension commitments, biggest borrower and debtor. And that's true of virtually every government in every country as well.

No wonder business leaders have had to evolve their concerns beyond tax policies and government regulations that affect only their industries and self-interests. In fact, business leaders have essentially had to become politicians themselves.

Some business leaders prefer to engage in battle against government policy makers or regulators through third parties like the Business Roundtable, the U.S. Chamber of Commerce, industry trade associations, and by using hired guns—law firms, lobbyists, and public affairs consultants. Increasingly, however, leaders are less skittish about speaking out in favor of or against public policies—or for or against the government leaders behind those policies. Maybe because they see it as their social responsibility or personal moral duty, but more likely it is because consumers are increasingly demanding action.

Paul Polman, the former CEO of Unilever, has been particularly outspoken in his speaking appearances at the World Economic Forum and other thought-leadership platforms on subjects ranging from obesity to global hunger. As he said, "The world we want is an enormous responsibility." Polman's activism evidently did not hurt Unilever's performance. Total shareholder return was up nearly 300 percent during his ten-year tenure as chief executive.

Under the leadership of longtime chief executive Bob Iger, even the Walt Disney Company, known for its family appeal and historical avoidance of politics, broke with tradition and became a critic of White House policies and communication. "The entry of the mild-mannered Iger and his squeaky-clean company into the arena shows how President Trump has a way of drawing people and corporations once considered apolitical into the red-hot center," according to the *New York Times.*

The article also noted that Iger found himself in "the middle of the culture wars that have broken out over [President Trump's] approach to race, the media, health care, climate change, and gun violence, not to mention the appropriateness of athletes' taking a knee in protest during the national anthem."

Iger told *New York Times* reporter Jim Rutenberg that he took a position on immigration in favor of the DACA (Deferred Action for Childhood Arrivals) program "because of how the issue affected the company"—meaning he supported access to all talented Americans, including those lacking "official" papers but who nonetheless consider the U.S. home and want to live and work there. He said he took a position on the Paris climate control accords for the same bottom-line reasons.

In his time at the helm of Apple, CEO Tim Cook has also taken many public positions. He was asked in a CNBC interview for his thoughts on corporate leaders who declined to attend CEO meetings at the White House in the early months of the Trump administration. "If you don't show up, I think that's the worst scenario," he said.

"Because then you are quiet, and this doesn't do your cause any good, or your point of view any good."

Apple has taken positions on public policies from immigration to pay equality. Cook probably has very good instincts—and advisers—about which topics to engage in without fear of retribution or negative consumer impact. He also may be one of those leaders who think that the CEO must personify the moral conscience of his or her organization—to stand up for what he or she believes is right. Perhaps it also helps to be in a state that is accustomed to outspoken politicians like California governor Gavin Newsom, U.S. House speaker Nancy Pelosi, House majority leader Kevin McCarthy, and U.S. senators Kamala Harris and Dianne Feinstein. Feinstein once remarked that "90 percent of leadership is the ability to communicate something people want." In other words, people listen and respond if there is a benefit, including the benefit of knowing a leader fully supports something you are passionate about.

Championing the Little Guy

Throughout its history Goldman Sachs has advised the U.S. government on policy matters related to public finance. Some of its leaders have taken high-level positions in governments—including former U.S. Treasury Secretaries Robert Rubin and Hank Paulson, and Mario Draghi as head of the European Central Bank. But policy commentary rose to a new level under a recent Goldman ex-CEO. Lloyd Blankfein spoke out on matters ranging from climate change to immigration, and LGBT rights to gender pay disparity. Yet he told Jim Cramer of CNBC that he preferred talking about issues he viewed in Goldman Sachs's "wheelhouse."

"I have to be a champion of our people, and I owe it to the body politic to comment where I have expertise," Blankfein said, "They can take my advice or not. I don't make [public policy] decisions, but I do give them my expertise."

Joseph Swedish, former CEO of Anthem Inc., was asked in an interview with the *Wall Street Journal* if CEOs should participate in public debates like healthcare reform. "Absolutely," Swedish answered. "We're leaders of companies that represent millions of Americans; in our case, forty million members. We believe we are their voice. And we should speak on their behalf."

Another company leader in the healthcare industry even stated his personal philosophy on speaking up on societal matters. Stanley M. Bergman, CEO of Henry Schein, an international distributor of healthcare products and services, highlighted his 1976 immigration to the U.S. from South Africa when he was honored as *Chief Executive* magazine's CEO of the Year in 2017.

"The country welcomed us with open arms," Bergman said. "We as business leaders have a responsibility to be engaged in the shaping of society. So here is my appeal to all business leaders: We cannot leave people behind. Too many in business have been too focused on going fast and not focused enough on going together. The result is a minority of huge beneficiaries and an increasingly vocal majority of those left behind. If we focus too much on the speed of change rather than ensuring that all benefit from change, then we risk greater disenfranchisement and civil dissent, which jeopardizes global stability and all democratic societies."

Bergman also spoke on that occasion about the importance of building bridges among political, business, religious, and cultural leaders—and to do so with civility rather than blasting rhetoric from behind institutional parapets. "Something greater than ourselves is at stake," Bergman added, quoting his hero, the late South African President Nelson Mandela: "You mustn't compromise your principles, but you mustn't humiliate the opposition. No one is more dangerous than one who is humiliated."

Trust and Public Engagement

In a speech at the Institute for PR's annual Distinguished Lecture, the CEO of global communications marketing firm Edelman underscored the benefits of business leaders as social activists. Richard Edelman said that engagement in public policy by business leaders "reflects the evolution of business as a positive force in society and calls for business to participate meaningfully in the continuous global conversation. Public engagement is policy and communications unified to realize the full aspirations of PR."

Edelman went on to note that the outcomes of public engagement could include "increased trust, changed behavior, deeper communities, and commercial success." Society's perceptions of the trust placed in public and private institutions is a hallmark of Edelman's annual Trust Barometer survey, now in its nineteenth year. The 2019 barometer found a spike in "trust inequality." According to its global survey, Edelman found that 75 percent of people trust "my employer" to do what is right, significantly more than NGOs (57 percent), business (56 percent), and media (47 percent).

Edelman might agree with the observation of former British Petroleum (BP) CEO, Sir John Browne. Browne argued in his book *Connect* that one strategy for building trust—corporate social responsibility—has failed because it has been disconnected from commercial activity and the needs of real people. "The connection between business and the world can only thrive if companies integrate societal and environmental issues deeply into their core business strategy and operations."

Of course, the global issue of climate change is the elephant in the room of energy company chiefs, as well as government leaders. Activist investors in 2019 coalesced to put forward a shareholders' resolution calling for BP to align its carbon emission goals with the 2015 Paris Agreement on climate change. Robert Dudley, BP's group chief executive since the aftermath of the company's Deepwater Horizon catastrophe, acted in a way that concerned shareholders and environmentalists could support. He tied the annual performance bonuses of all thirty-six thousand BP executives and employees to the company's targeted reduction of greenhouse gas emissions.

BP believes it can reduce carbon emissions by 3.5 million tons by 2025 while continuing to find cleaner and better sources of energy to meet the demands of a growing global population. "Building an emissions reduction target into the reward of people throughout BP further underlines the importance we place on this work," Dudley said. "We expect it will catalyze even more ideas and activity and support BP playing our part in addressing the dual challenge."

Whether you are a business, government, or civic leader, the goal should be the same: try to solve societal problems with long-term solutions, preferably solutions that make a force-multiplying impact greater than the financial and volunteer resources devoted to it. You have to choose issues that fit your company or that are relevant to the interests of your employees and associates. Focus is necessary. Sometimes events influence executive decisions.

Dick's Sporting Goods did just that when it decided to stop selling guns in its stores in the aftermath of the massacre of seventeen people at a Parkland, Florida, high school in 2018. Later, the company destroyed all unsold assault weapons pulled from the store's retail shelves and cases. Dick's CEO, Edward Stack, demonstrated courage in entering the polarized gun debate in the dramatic way. Interestingly, just days before the Parkland shooting, Stack lamented in full-page newspaper ads that "today our world, our country, even our communities are as divided as they have ever been." But he wasn't talking about gun control. He was celebrating the start of the 2018 Winter Olympic Games in South Korea, noting that pervasive forces of divisiveness in society "can't break the human spirit." Stack would later tell shareholders and analysts that its stance on guns had an impact in the company's 2018 drop in sales. He said some gun owners likely stopped patronizing Dick's stores.

Leadership Is Service

Former Ohio governor John Kasich addressed leadership problem solving in his book *Two Paths.* "For too long, politicians have been making promises based on polling or what was politically expedient. That is not leadership. Leadership is the willingness to walk a lonely road with a team of people with their eyes fixed on the horizon, focused on solving problems and healing our country. Leading is serving."

Leon Panetta serves as a consistent example of a true leader. His communication style projects credibility and confidence, and he offers specific bipartisan actions without fear of criticism from political opponents and commentators. I have had the pleasure of meeting with Panetta on many occasions, including at events and forums held by the Panetta Institute for Public Policy in

Monterey, California. The institute's mission is to help prepare young people for careers in public and government service.

Panetta is an estimable mentor in that regard. In addition to a long career in Washington as a congressman, Panetta served President Clinton as the director of the Office of Management and Budget and as White House chief of staff. He later served under President Obama as CIA director and Secretary of Defense. He is known for his candor and wit and is often sought by the news media for commentary and perspective on major policy debates in the nation's capital.

In his book *Worthy Fights: A Memoir of Leadership in War and Peace,* Panetta criticized policy makers who say that they cannot be held responsible for political and polarity inaction spurred by historic ideological differences in America. "The people of this country are more united than it seems on what is needed to secure their families and give their children a better life," he wrote. "It is the responsibility of leaders to lead America in that direction, not to score points or win reelection. Because without leadership, there is crisis."

I believe that the 2016 U.S. presidential election was a reckoning in which a high percentage of voters rejected tradition and convention and the tired rhetoric of career politicians. For many of them, the thinking was, "I have heard this before. What are you doing specifically to help me?" That was the issue in the minds of millions as they watched political debates and observed the election, either by participating in rallies and town hall meetings or monitoring news reports. As a result, a political outsider like Trump was elected, despite the odds against him even making it through the Republican primaries.

But I take a broader view. I believe Trump's election was

based more on what voters were not getting. In a postelection article for *PRWeek*, I wrote, "A bigger conclusion will be that voters—once again—didn't like the product that politics is delivering, and that product is government itself. Millions of voters certainly don't like the price we are paying and the value we are receiving for federal or local government services. And after all, for most people, government taxes and service fees are the biggest item in their annual household budgets. When something is the biggest, fixed annual cost that you and your family *must* pay, you are bound to periodically demand your money's worth. We not only pay dearly for services performed by government today, but we also pay for all the government mistakes of the past and the enormous debt service on past and future borrowing."

I also noted that we have choices. "Elections are the rare time, in a marketing sense, where people get to make a choice among competitive political options. This time, one presidential candidate, rightly or wrongly, told voters they were getting screwed by their own government, and that he would find ways to put a stop to it. He now owns that promise . . . to fix things."

The Global Stage

All politics may be local, but leaders who take positions on global issues are often seeking international platforms. There are many places for leaders to make speeches and influence public policy, but few are as impactful as the World Economic Forum and its annual confab in the Switzerland ski resort village of Davos.

Most of the world's problems have been discussed in Davos,

where leadership and communication are notably disconnected. The problem is that few of the proposed solutions in Davos are ever acted on. Despite four days of brilliant rhetoric by countless WEF speakers and expert panelists, not much of substance happens after the government, business, and NGO leaders head home. Davos on a grand scale is like a company meeting where everyone in the room discusses a plan of action, then walks away without the authority, accountability, or even the inclination to follow through on the plan.

The WEF has always had the potential to influence transformative, long-term progress in the world. And, in doing so, to be a model for other international institutions. It is a good thing when critics challenge the WEF to focus on tangible actions that may benefit the many versus the privileged few. In fact, there are many who believe the WEF best serves billionaires, fast-emerging economies, and the multinational companies and NGOs that benefit from global trade, commerce, and the gradual redistribution of prosperity. This does not mean the World Economic Forum is a waste of time. Hardly.

If you have attended, you know that it presents great value in terms of what you can learn there and whom you might meet. For leaders, new perspectives and new relationships (particularly those that are influential) matter greatly. The forum is also a remarkable conference for listening to experts—everyone from economic scholars to revolutionary thinkers to entrepreneurs—debate potential solutions to common economic and human problems. Those subjects, along with other issues that run the gamut from A to Z, get dawn-to-dusk attention at Davos.

I have attended the WEF in Davos five times and have been a speaker at WEF conferences in India, South Africa, Peru, the

United Arab Emirates, and various European countries. Because I also had important clients attending these meetings, particularly the annual conference in Davos, I was often working fifteen-hour days to make sure those clients were prepared for media interviews and meetings with government or NGO leaders, CEOs, business partners, and prospects. My experiences in Davos were always enlightening and positive, and they often resulted in relationships with people whose achievements truly have made a difference for communities and for humanity as a whole.

After the 2017 meeting, Gerard Baker, the former editor in chief of the *Wall Street Journal,* commented that Davos is a talkfest for aristocrats, elites, and globetrotting leaders. But I disagree, at least in part. It is also for NGO leaders, start-up entrepreneurs, authors, leading academics, medical researchers, and non-celebrities. The collaborative spirit makes it possible to have memorable, earnest conversations with Davos A-listers. And where else could a businessperson talk to sovereign leaders without the presence of their security teams, CEOs without their handlers, or U.S. senators without an appointment?

Steve Barrett, editor in chief of *PRWeek* U.S., said this after attending his first WEF in 2019: "At the end of my first week in Davos, I was left to reflect that, once you've cut through the inevitable BS, grandstanding, ostentation, and showboating, a lot of business gets done here and the time is used very effectively by business, government, and nonprofits."

In addition to being at the forefront of corporate activism, the WEF has provided an arena for leaders to communicate with social activists. As a result, it has always had the potential to influence transformative, long-term progress in the world, and in doing so, to serve as a model for other international institutions.

Nonetheless, it is good that Baker and others have challenged the WEF to focus on actions that will benefit the many and not just the privileged few.

Speaking Truth to Power

Since the earliest days of my career, I have been fascinated by people who have stood up and spoken truth to power. My early experience as a Chicago-based political reporter included covering the campaign of a true underdog, a congressman named Harold Washington. He was attempting to become the first black mayor of Chicago. Washington spoke truth to power with eloquence and a sharp sense of humor, castigating the old ways of bossism and racial politics at city hall.

But the odds were against him. He was taking on an incumbent mayor who was the city's first female mayor and had the backing of its longtime Democratic political machine. And there was another formidable candidate in Richard M. Daley, the eldest son of Chicago's six-time elected mayor. Yet Washington's presence in the race spurred massive voter registration and turnout in his favor. He won the election. (Daley later would become mayor a few years after Washington died while serving his second term in office. Today, Chicago has its first African-American woman as mayor: Lori Lightfoot.)

Today, anyone with a Twitter account or a Facebook page can express their feelings toward politicians, corporations, church leaders, and other wielders of institutional power. Brave individuals do it under their own names, while others hide behind anonymous personas and creative usernames. It is commonplace in democratic societies to protest this way, but far riskier and rarer in authoritarian states where traditional news media are suppressed and social media closely surveilled.

Nonetheless, great social and political movements have been started by emerging leaders and dissidents opposing the inequalities of the status quo, or in rallying people on behalf of civil liberties, human rights, and the rule of law. Their manifestos and call-to-action communications have been widely distributed over social media platforms and by old-fashioned word of mouth in places where social media penetration is lower.

Truth-to-power confrontations between the leaders of the haves and the have-nots have occurred since ancient times: Moses versus Pharaoh Ramses; Jesus Christ versus the Pharisees and the Romans; Martin Luther versus the Catholic Church; Thomas Paine versus the British government and its colonial loyalists; Gandhi versus India's British rulers; the *Washington Post* versus the Nixon White House; Nelson Mandela versus South Africa's apartheid upholders; and the Tiananmen Square protesters versus the Chinese government.

One of those Tiananmen Square protesters, in fact, went on to win a Nobel Peace Prize. He was Liu Xiaobo, a Chinese human rights activist who began speaking out against the government while a lecturer at Beijing Normal University.

For his participation in the march on Tiananmen Square in 1989, Liu received a twenty-one-month prison sentence. He continued his dissent after his release and eventually signed the controversial democratic manifesto known as Charter 8, which China's liberal intelligentsia was preparing to submit to the government in Beijing. Chinese police later arrested Liu on suspicion of "inciting subversion of state power," and a court convicted him in 2008, resulting in another prison sentence, this time for eleven years.

Every day in the streets or public squares of some city, protesters rally around leaders armed with nothing but a microphone or a megaphone. This is another dynamic of leadership communication—the kind that stirs people from states of apathy or helplessness and empowers them to use their voices, their ballots, and their boycotts to effect change for the better.

Leaders of dissident movements have taken down unpopular governments in some cases, many winning a Nobel Peace Prize as a result of their activism, including Lech Walesa, Nelson Mandela, and Desmond Tutu. Others have protested while exiled from their homelands.

Shirin Ebadi of Iran is one such exile. The founder of the Defenders of Human Rights Center, Ebadi received the 2003 Nobel Peace Prize for her efforts on behalf of democracy and human rights, and was the first Iranian woman to serve as a judge. She also acted as a human rights lawyer to defend clients unfairly prosecuted by the state, including dozens of women arrested for opposing discriminatory gender laws.

After the disputed presidential election of 2009, when President Mahmoud Ahmadinejad's re-election triggered protests and demands for a recount, Ebadi went into self-imposed exile in England. Like other dissidents in exile around the world, she continued to communicate from afar on behalf of the Green Movement and human rights for Iranians.

Garry Kasparov, the world-class chess master, is a Russian dissident who has long been a leading critic of Kremlin ideology and policies. Kasparov is also known as one of the world's all-time greatest chess champions, even though he has admitted that "chess is mental torture." But in politics he has been frustrated by one of the toughest opponents of his career: Vladimir Putin, whom he has compared to a mafia godfather and a gangster.

Kasparov tried to reform the Russian government through conventional means, founding political organizations and coalitions to challenge Putin's power and control. In the end, however, his plan to run against President Dmitry Medvedev in the 2008 Russian presidential election was foiled when a harassment campaign—which he alleged was run out of the Kremlin—forced him to withdraw from the election.

Kasparov expressed the futility of challenging Putin this way: "The only successor to President Putin is President Putin himself."

When a Leader Disappoints

One of the best-known dissidents of the past few decades is Aung San Suu Kyi, yet another recipient of the Nobel Peace Prize, which she was awarded in 1991. Her storied life as a democratic activist in Myanmar inspired the people of her country to protest in the streets and turn out for democratic elections to replace ruling juntas. "You should never let your fears prevent you from doing what you know is right," she once said. It is a remark that could well stand as a universal theme marking many pivotal moments in history when leaders in power, or leaders opposing authority, made the choice to either speak out against injustice and criminal activity or keep silent.

Aung San Suu Kyi is a former dissident who came to know that actual leadership of a nation can bring stinging criticism and derision on the global stage. After heroically speaking out against the ruling class during many years of living under house arrest, she assumed power herself in a landslide election in 2015.

By 2017, however, she found herself accused of failing to prevent acts of genocide against the Rohingya, a Muslim ethnic minority in Myanmar. As a Buddhist, she has been accused of racism and ethnic cleansing. In fact, the genocide taking place in Myanmar has compelled some nations to condemn her, and the United Nations has talked of holding her and her government accountable for the deaths and expulsion of the Rohingya. There has even been talk of rescinding her Nobel Peace Prize, and other organizations have already revoked honors bestowed upon her while she was a human rights warrior. Has Aung San Suu Kyi created the very fear in Myanmar that she encouraged her people to fearlessly transcend in opposing the prior regime? Only time will tell if this onetime human rights idol will be found guilty of crimes of humanity against her own countrymen and political supporters. Either way, her example shows that the actions taken by leaders while in positions of authority can undo all of the moral courage and integrity they demonstrated (and communicated) as activists.

Coincidentally, the controversy surrounding Aung San Suu Kyi came at the same time that women were standing up to publicly vilify sexual harassment and the mistreatment of women in Hollywood and other industries. Women ranging from famous actresses to former Capitol Hill staffers stepped up to name names and add fuel to the #MeToo campaign. The movement gained momentum as more and more women came forward with allegations of being sexually harassed and humiliated by men who used the power of industry position for advantage.

When a Leader Inspires

One of the more impassioned speeches on the #MeToo subject was given by Oprah Winfrey at the 2018 Golden Globe Awards ceremony, when she accepted the Cecil B. DeMille Lifetime Achievement honor. "What I know for sure is that speaking your truth is the most powerful tool we all have," Winfrey told the audience. "And I'm especially proud and inspired by all the women who have felt strong enough and empowered enough to speak up and share their personal stories. Each of us in this room are celebrated because of the stories that we tell, and this year we became the story. But it's not just a story affecting the entertainment industry. It's one that transcends any culture, geography, race, religion, politics, or workplace."

Winfrey added a tribute to all the women who suffered their indignities in silence: "I want tonight to express gratitude to all the women who have endured years of abuse and assault because they, like my mother, had children to feed and bills to pay and dreams to pursue. They're the women whose names we'll never know. They are domestic workers and farmworkers. They are working in factories and they work in restaurants and they're in academia, engineering, medicine, and science. They're part of the world of tech and in politics and business. They're our athletes in the Olympics and they're our soldiers in the military."

Winfrey's speech set Twitter aflame with calls for her to run for president in 2020. Commentators viewed Winfrey's speech as a promise to a generation of young girls that better days lie ahead, especially if influential women continued to speak out against what is wrong in society.

U.S. Senator Kirsten Gillibrand, a New York Democrat and onetime 2020 presidential candidate, framed this leadership-communication responsibility and activism another way: "When a woman has the opportunity to speak truth to power, it's important that she does, even if it's just trying to get a crosswalk in her neighborhood. That's how social change happens!"

Leadership requires courage in both action and communications. To mobilize people in a social cause or a political movement, words matter. Leaders do not need complicated language to inspire people to reach their full potential in achieving great things and solving problems. Simple words can be powerful. Stories illuminating wisdom and leadership by example are powerful, too.

As Winston Churchill once said, "All the great things are simple, and many can be expressed in a single word: freedom, justice, honor, duty, mercy, hope."

Communication is central to leadership. It can be the difference-making factor in mission clarity, bringing meaning and purpose to human performance, and balancing the scales of opportunity and risk.

For leaders now and to be, Talk Is Chief.

Key Insights and Observations

- We are living in a new era where corporate leaders have joined NGOs and social activists in taking public positions on government policies affecting their employees, customers, and segments of the public for which they are most concerned.
- Courageous business leaders and political leaders alike can be activists for good public policy and advocates for social change.
- Speaking truth to power is an ancient practice. But today great movements can grow rapidly through social media and technology that catalyzes dissent and demands for change.

IS IT BEFORE , OR BEFORE ?
Hafeez.

9

Final Thoughts: Words as Weapons and Personal Communication Style

"The difference between the right word and the almost right word is the difference between lightning and the lightning bug."

—**Mark Twain**, American writer and humorist

A leader gets up early, rising in her home, hotel room, or maybe a flat-bed seat on an overnight flight. As the day begins, the leader's head is full of words—word clouds that surfaced amid fitful sleep and subconscious states. Action words like *meet, call, build, buy, fix, innovate, invest, negotiate, collaborate, intervene, arbitrage, commend, correct, organize, energize, hire, terminate.* It feels like waking up in a Nike commercial. But the leader's life is about daily grinding and long-term progress—questions, directions, decisions, and actions amplified through action verbs.

Today's leaders are like warlords of old, except they are *wordlords*—words being their weapons of greatest utility. (Take away the first "s" in *swords* and you're left with *words.*) Words have started—and ended—wars. Leaders speak, tweet, email, text, and sometimes shout thousands of words every day. Words are the interactive elements in their ever-evolving ecosystems. But just because a leader talks, it doesn't necessarily mean his stakeholders are responding affirmatively, making their commitments to the leader's agenda. This is especially true in organizations in which people have lost their trust in institutional leadership.

Words and Pictures Matter Greatly When Trying to Inspire People

In her weekly column in the *Wall Street Journal,* Peggy Noonan wrote about what good leaders do. "Great leaders are capable of arguing for the things they believe in," she wrote. "They can make the case. ...Their words aren't emotional, as politicians tend to be now in an attempt to make a sated audience feel something." She said that when leaders employ logic and fact, they can make people "feel something," like respect and "membership in a community of thought and belief."

Which is why I cringe when I see leaders giving presentations with language that sounds straight out of a Securities and Exchange Commission filing. But words alone—even Mark Twain's "right" words—will not make a difference unless they amplify the strategic plans, decisions, and actions that go with them. Together, the right words and the right actions are a powerful combination.

In 2016 I published in a public relations industry magazine an article entitled "How Leaders Can Influence Top Performance, Risk Identification, and Trust-Building for Their Organizations." A key point of the article: "Corporate directors and shareholders still assess performance primarily on business and financial results. But they also have an obligation to evaluate leaders, particularly chief executives, on their ability to inspire organizations to achieve great feats—like rallying people to make game-changing products, or to deliver superb customer experiences. Leadership communication is as vital to organizational success as smart people, technology advantage, and healthy capital funding."

I also noted that "leaders are expected to be dynamic communicators because of the iconic stages on which they perform. But they need not be naturally gifted, just thoughtful about what they say and how they say it. Coaching from skilled practitioners can ensure their leaders communicate frequently, unambiguously, positively, memorably, and contextually."

So what makes a leader a good communicator? Leaders must be visible communicators—in good times and bad, in person or webcasted. That's how to keep people focused on the goals, values, and ultimate "we matter" purpose of the organization.

A leader should have a personal style of communicating, one that relies on uncomplicated language, a strong voice, and a well-paced delivery. I have witnessed some very smart leaders who think they have to talk rapidly because that is the speed at which their brains work. I always tell them to slow it down, to pause and emphasize the most important messages in their talks and presentations.

Early on I learned that to get the story in your own voice, you must have something newsworthy or of informational value, and say it concisely and genuinely. This is especially true today in a world where five-second TV sound bites and tweets provide colorful sidebars and sometimes even news headlines.

Tongue Twisters

A leader's words leave a permanent trail, just as hardened lava flows around a dormant volcano. In this age of digital permanency, any public person's rhetorical footprint lives forever in cyberspace. And any leader likely offers a good deal of searchable content. With just a few clicks, what was said last year or tweeted this morning is instantly available. If something became part of the digital record in the last twenty years, there is a good chance it can be found on any search engine. Twenty years from now, people will be able to easily find a speech a leader gave at a conference last week.

In today's hyperconnected world, a leader's words can travel far beyond intended context to other audiences, sometimes with unintended consequences. Even worse are words meant to praise—but that come out wrong and are remembered as a gaffe or faux pas.

Sometimes an organization's leader fumbles the chance to communicate a memorable message at a watershed moment in a career. For example, in March 1992, during the primary season, President George H. W. Bush was scheduled to visit Chicago for a presidential primary election campaign stop. A colleague of mine had a brother who worked in the Bush administration, and the brother had reached out for help in finding a friendly organization for the President to address the afternoon before the primary.

After some political calculations, we chose the Polish National Alliance (PNA), which represented a GOP-leaning demographic. As part of the planning and logistics, I told the president of the PNA that I would draft his remarks to introduce President Bush. When I presented the draft, however, he rejected it, saying it was not in his voice or style, and that he would rewrite it himself.

On the day of the event, the PNA leader stepped to the podium to introduce the President, who stood directly behind him. His remarks were arranged around the themes of freedom, ethnic heritage, the end of the Cold War, and the challenges Poland faced in its first years of liberation from Soviet rule. None of the national pool reporters assigned to follow Bush were paying much attention to his monotonal introduction. Until, that is, he reached his final sentence: "Ladies and gentlemen, at this time I am most privileged to introduce our number one freedom farter—*fighter*—and the most popular American in Poland, the President of the United States, George Bush."

I wasn't sure I had heard him correctly. But just behind me, Sam Donaldson, the White House correspondent for ABC News, said, "Did he just say *freedom farter*?" Another pool reporter confirmed it. For the poor PNA leader, it was a moment reminiscent of eight-year-old Ralphie saying the *F* word while helping his father change a tire in the movie version of Jean Shepherd's *A Christmas Story*. The PNA leader's face burned with humiliation as the President, suppressing a chuckle, took the podium.

The point of this tale is that even when you want to sound authentic, it pays to work closely with someone who can coach you on your delivery. Otherwise tongue-twisting alliteration can earn you an unintended outcome that will live on forever in a C-SPAN video on YouTube. Leaders need to give people something memorable to take away from their communications. And while the PNA leader did indeed leave words that were memorable, they were the wrong kind of memorable.

Tricks of the Trade

Whether giving a formal speech or a casual talk, I follow the same simple guidelines:

- **Memorable takeaways:** People tend to forget 90 percent of what they hear and read after a few days. But with every communication, there should be strong, transcendent language that is memorable and that speaks to organizational mission and purpose. You know what I mean if you have been to a Broadway or West End musical and walked out lamenting, "I can't remember any of the music and lyrics. There were no hummable tunes." That does not happen when people see some of the great modern shows or hear the classics of Rodgers and Hammerstein, Stephen Sondheim, Andrew Lloyd Webber, and other great composers and lyricists. Good communication is like a hummable tune. Memorable and, at its best, motivating.

- **An authentic voice:** If a prepared speech or town hall–style remarks do not sound like the leader, listeners tune out. People want authenticity, and authenticity shines through in the cadence and word choices with which the leader is comfortable. It should feel like a conversation with the audience rather than a lecture. It helps to speak directly to specific people in the audience and to make eye contact. Get them nodding in approval and ready to applaud—and not just on cue because you said something worth applauding. Pause for emphasis. Repeat an important sentence to underscore a point if that seems the best way to communicate a key message.

- **Visual storytelling:** I stopped using PowerPoint slides heavy on words and numbers long ago. They're boring. For multigeneration audiences, internal or external, I tend toward big pictures, cartoons, and graphics to illustrate the messages I want to convey. People grasp pictures much more quickly on a big screen than they do text. Even more, if they're focused on reading copy, they are less likely to take in what you're saying. With Projeqt and other similar software you can embed live tweets, Flickr images, YouTube or Vimeo videos, audio, and interactive maps within presentations. Pictures and other visuals are also key to simplicity: turning the complex into the understandable and memorable. For example, the old photographic tactic of posing politicians next to ceiling-high stacks of government regulations to demonstrate an overregulated society. As Einstein once said, "If you can't explain it simply, you don't understand it well enough." Today, with computer-generated graphics, any visualization is possible to better communicate an idea, policy position, or product concept.

- **Big data:** Data communicated by leaders can overwhelm, even when supported with pictures and charts. Infographics and visuals make the complex easier to understand.

- **Know your audience:** What do they already know? What are their expectations? What is their relationship to you and your organization? The better you understand your audience, the better you can connect. Speaking in a large conference room or from a ballroom stage works best when you understand your audience and can connect with them. When speaking to strangers, that means finding faces in the crowd (perhaps those familiar from pre-speech research) with whom you can make eye contact and speak to directly. When speaking to known-by-name employees and associates, the same point regarding eye contact applies, but even better are specific shout-outs in which you acknowledge individuals, teams, and their achievements. That always gets the attention of an audience, who will be listening intently for those mentioned and those not.

- **Humor:** I open talks with humorous stories designed to connect with the audience. While giving a speech in a Midwestern city, for example, I told the audience how, on an earlier business trip to their city, I embarrassed myself in the hotel restaurant when the candle on my table set my newspaper on fire. The self-deprecating tale broke the ice and the audience was laughing and attentive as I proceeded with my talk. I got similar laughs at a World Economic Forum conference in India when I told the largely Indian audience how much I appreciated being in a country where long surnames like mine were common. That said, make sure your anecdotes translate culturally. In preparing for a speech to management professionals in Sweden, I considered opening with the words of Casey Stengel, the legendary American baseball manager: "The secret of managing is to keep the five guys who hate you away from the guys who are undecided." Ultimately, however, I decided the audience would not be familiar with Stengel, much as they might appreciate his humor.

- **Repetition:** As a journalist and communicator, I learned never to bury your lede. In other words, lead with the headline and the messages you most want people to take away from your speech or town hall dialogue. Building up to the conclusion runs the risk of people tuning out early and not paying any attention to your takeaways when you finally get to them. Jack Welch got it right when he advised that repetition is the key. Start with your main themes and come back to them—as eloquently as possible—over and over again. Martin Luther King used anaphoric repetition to emphasize such core messages as "let freedom ring." (History will attest to the fact that it worked well for Dr. King.)

- **Timing:** Considering the age we live in, in which digital devices compete for every minute of our attention, less is more. No one wants to sit through a half-hour monologue unless it is an absolutely fascinating subject. If you have twenty-five minutes of really good subject matter, try to get it down to fifteen to twenty minutes. Your audience will respond better.

- **Smile:** Too many leaders step onto a stage or up to a podium looking as though their best friend had just died. Which is fine if you are giving a eulogy. Or delivering bad news. But for most other occasions, smiling at your audience when you take the stage will assuage some of the nervous anxiety you are likely to feel. It will also communicate to the audience that you are happy to be there and ready to engage and even energize them. Before any speech or presentation, just remember: the audience wants to like you.

- **Practice and rehearse:** Present your remarks to a small test audience from within your organization, one that can provide candid feedback and expose you to questions your audience is likely to ask. A practice session like this can help polish your remarks, build your confidence, and avoid giving the wrong

> answer to a question. Communication and marketing pros labor to construct messages very carefully and then pressure test the assertions, promises, and facts underlying them in advance of leaders employing those narratives for public consumption. Almost every question directed at a leader can both be answered and linked to core messages. That's not spin; that's leadership taking command of communication opportunities.

In addition to these practical tips, leaders must have a repertoire of go-to messages on hand. That does not mean they can't go off-message occasionally to add color, context, or personal connection to the content they are communicating. Leaders both can and should. But only if such spontaneity comes across as genuine. And segue back on message.

Leaders should understand the great opportunities—and occasional risks—that clear, brain-tingling communication presents for the nations, organizations, and people they lead. In particular, leadership communication offers a big opportunity to bring the best out in people, challenging them to do their best work or to rise up and confront extreme adversity with spirited countermeasures.

We expect a lot from our leaders. We expect them to make bold plans and know how to achieve them. Expect them to light the way with strategic beacons for others to follow. Expect them to see future opportunities and take calculated yet doable risks. We want them to provide job and career opportunities—and financial security—for employees. We hope they can identify and fix bad situations before they turn into crises, or at least restore normality, harmony, and prosperity when troubling times occur. And we expect them to think big thoughts and ideas—but also be able to express them in simple, understandable language.

As I told that New York University business class of future entrepreneurs, accountants, and business managers: "You are all in communications."

Acknowledgments

I have had occasional bucket list adventures in my life, like getting into a shark cage off the coast of South Africa with Great Whites circling the chummed waters around the boat. Or skydiving for the first time over a Colorado plain, praying the parachute would open properly. In both cases, one such thrilling experience was quite enough.

Early in my career as a journalist I wrote hundreds of newspaper articles and columns, including a few that won awards. And in my public relations business career, I drafted many commentaries, speeches, white papers, video scripts, and news announcements for clients.

So, when it came to writing my first book, I thought my literary abilities would make the task easy. It wasn't.

Winston Churchill was spot on when he said the adventure of writing a book "becomes a master, then it becomes a tyrant. The last phase is that just as you are about to be reconciled to your servitude, you kill the monster and fling him to the public." And he, of course, was a prolific author.

It's only proper to credit the many people who helped me get *Talk Is Chief: Leadership, Communications & Credibility in a High-Stakes World* to the finish line. I'll start out with author and marketing consultant extraordinaire Andy Cunningham, who led me to the folks at Silicon Valley Press—Joe DiNucci, Atiya Dwyer, and Lauren Cuthbert. They helped edit and polish the first drafts of the book. Through that process they reminded me of lessons I learned back in journalism school—including less is better. Together we eliminated parts of the manuscript that did not serve the interests of readers.

I sincerely thank the team at RosettaBooks: publisher and long-time book industry veteran Arthur Klebanoff, and his estimable team of Brian Skulnik, Michelle Weyenberg, and Emily Proano. They have been terrific in every way.

I also received some early coaching from Karl Weber, a veteran book editor, and from Rafe Sagalyn, a top literary agent. Both provided blunt and welcomed advice on how to differentiate the book from the broad category of leadership themes and topics. In that regard, I thank David Greising, a long-time business journalist, author, and colleague at the Better Government Association, for pointing me to Weber. And to Candy Lee, a professor at the Medill School of Journalism, Media, Integrated Marketing Communications. Candy introduced me to Sagalyn.

There are many to thank for reading parts of the book and providing sage advice and encouragement. Joseph "Andy" Hays, a former client at Tribune Company, read early manuscript chapters and made poignant recommendations. Janet Robinson, the former CEO of The New York Times Company, told me the book would have real value to current and future leaders. I am also extremely grateful to those who took the time to read parts of the book and afterward endorse it. Their gracious comments about *Talk Is Chief* convinced me that I truly had stories, career lessons, and contemporary observations worth sharing. And friends such as Scott Nations, John Anderson, Gary Karrass, Tim Franklin, Rita Dragonette, Trevor Mathias, David Kohn, Greg Burns, Sol Lieberman, Jonathan Copulsky, Belinda L. Clarke, and others who provided helpful advice on the book and publication-related activities.

No one reaches this point of recollecting about career events without remembering all those who mentored, supported, and worked alongside of him—colleagues, clients, and professors—during a professional career that spanned decades. I am especially appreciative of the people and friends, past and present, at FleishmanHillard and Omnicom Group, where I spent the majority of my agency life. There were several mentors who had a tremendous influence on my career, including Al Golin and Tom Harris who founded GolinHarris (now called Golin), and former Golin CEO Rich Jernstedt; John Graham, the longtime CEO and chairman of FleishmanHillard; and FH executives Rick Sullivan and Bill Anderson.

As with any achievement, there are too many to thank who in some way influenced my career and this work. But I plan to thank as many of them as I can in future days.

Finally, I wish to thank Sue Kiner. She's my wife, best friend, and my better three-quarters. She frequently identifies important considerations that others miss. Her creative talents, intuition, and judgment have made a difference—for this book and generally in inspiring me to raise my expectations and never to be daunted. She has made countless good suggestions that benefited my career, enlightened me, and enriched my life. In due time I believe she will add to our home library a book of her own.

Bibliography and Further Reading

Introduction

"Communication from the CEO's perspective—an Underestimated Challenge?" Egon Zehnder, 2011 survey of CEOs in Germany.

Gladwell, Malcolm. *Outliers: The Story of Success.* New York, NY: Little, Brown and Company, 2008.

Chapter 1

"Employee Engagement on the Rise in the U.S." Gallup.com poll August 26, 2018.

"Ketchum Leadership Communication Monitor (KLCM)." conducted with 3,000 respondents in 2015 and 2016 by the Omnicom firm Ketchum.

Global Relevance Review, Golin in partnership with the University of Southern California Annenberg School for Journalism and Communications, 2017 survey of 13,000 people on four continents.

"Global CEO Survey." PwC in 2017 reported that 58 percent of CEOs surveyed "worried that lack of trust in business would harm their company's growth." That figure was up 21 percent from 2013.

Nocera, Joe. "Ford Sees New CEO as Second Coming of Alan Mulally." *Bloomberg News,* May 23, 2017.

Lutz, Bob. "Mark Fields Was Old-fashioned CEO." *CNBC Squawk Box*, May 24, 2017.

Neff, Thomas J., and James M. Citrin. *Lessons from the Top: the 50 Most Successful Business Leaders in America—and What You Can Learn from Them.* New York: Currency/Doubleday, 1999.

Modzelewski, Jack. "The Power of Communications." *CEO Today*, 2003.

"Online Extra: Jeff Bezos on Word-of-Mouth Power." July 2004 *Bloomberg BusinessWeek* interview with Bezos on Amazon's brand resurgence.

Beck, Scott. "Why CEO Really Means Being Chief Communication Officer." *Entrepreneur*, August 23, 2016.

Sonnenfeld, Jeffrey. "Back to the Future: How 40 Years has Changed the CEO Post." *Chief Executive*, March 9, 2017.

Chapter 2

"Spotlight on PepsiCo CEO Indra Nooyi." *The CEO Magazine*, April 12, 2018.

"Jack Ma, a Tech Boom Showman." *Wall Street Journal*, September 11, 2018.

Gerstner, Lou. "The Culture Ate Our Corporate Reputation." *Wall Street Journal*, October 3, 2016.

Kraemer, Harry M. *From Values to Action: The Four Principles of Values-Based Leadership*. San Francisco, CA: Jossey-Bass, 2011.

Jargon, Julie. "Chipotle CEO Says No to Breakfast, Yes to Longer Hours." *Wall Street Journal*, April 28, 2018.

Ascending to the C-Suite, McKinsey & Company study, April 2015.

Eberwein, Elise. "Why the Chief Communications Officer is Pivotal to the CEO, Especially a New One." *Chief Executive*, September 11, 2016.

Sheffer, Gary. "What Every Company Needs to Know to Keep a Good Reputation." *Fortune*, March 18, 2016.

Chapter 3

Goldman, Jeremy. "13 Insightful Quotes from Intel Visionary Andy Grove." *Inc.*, 2016.

Lewis, Michael. *The Big Short.* New York: W.W. Norton & Company, 2010.

Modzelewski, Jack. "Armstrong Ignored Comms Lessons from Earlier in His Career." *PRWeek*, January 18, 2013.

do Rego Barros, Paulino. "On Behalf of Equifax, I'm Sorry." *Wall Street Journal*, Sept. 27, 2017.

Chapter 4

McAvoy, Audrey, and Jennifer Kelleher. "'We Made a Mistake' Hawaii Sends False Missile Alert." *Associated Press*, January 13, 2018.

Paulson, Henry M. *On the Brink: Inside the Race to Stop the Collapse of the Global Financial System.* New York, NY: Business Plus Hachette Book Group, 2010.

"Risk Map 2019." Control Risks.

Singer, Mark. "Stringer's Way: Can Sony's British CEO save an ailing brand?" *New Yorker*, May 28, 2006.

Reinhold, Robert. "California City's 2nd Disaster in 2 Weeks." *New York Times*, May 26, 1989.

Chapter 5

Walton, Sam, with John Huey. *Sam Walton: Made in America.* New York, NY: Doubleday, 1992.

Bradberry, Travis. "8 Secrets of Great Communicators." *Forbes*, July 19, 2018.

Weber Shandwick with KRC Research. "Report from the Buy Side." 2017.

Gallo, Carmine. "Richard Branson Explains Why Storytelling Is Your Competitive Advantage." *Forbes*, October 17, 2017.

Ruffo, Jillian. "Reese Witherspoon Is the New Face (and Storyteller-in-Chief) of Elizabeth Arden." *People*, March 30, 2017.

Abbey, Alison. "CBS This Morning Co-host Norah O'Donnell on Truth in Journalism and Sunday Traditions." *Parade*, February 9, 2018.

Pew Research Center, "American Trends Panel." 2017.

Chapter 6

Barrett, Steve. "The Road Ahead in 2019." *PRWeek*, December 21, 2018.

Montgomery, Walter G. "How CEOs Can Adopt a Modern 21st-century Approach to Communication." *Knowledge@Wharton*, August 17, 2015.

Margaritis, William. "Lessons Learned in Building a Successful Career." Speech.

Samson, Dave. "A future of opportunity for chief communications officers." *PRWeek*, April 27, 2016.

Olson, Nels, Beth Fowler, and Richard Marshall. "The Chief Communications Officer: 2015 Survey and Findings Among the Fortune 500." Korn Ferry Institute, July 28, 2015.

Whitacre, Edward with Lesley Cauley. *American Turnaround: Reinventing AT&T and GM and the Way We Do Business in the USA*. New York, NY: Business Plus, 2013.

Chapter 7

Seetharaman, Deepa. "Instagram CEO on Stories: Don't Call It a Copycat." *Wall Street Journal*, May 30, 2017.

Gallo, Carmine. "How Starbucks CEO Howard Schultz Inspired Us to Dream Bigger." *Forbes*, December 2, 2016.

Galloway, Scott. *The Four: The Hidden DNA of Apple, Amazon, Facebook, and Google*. New York, NY: Portfolio, 2017.

Orwell, George. *1984*. London: Secker & Warburg, 1949.

Kirkham, Chris. "Is This Hotel an Airbnb Killer?" *Wall Street Journal*, September 15, 2017.

"Omnicom Group Inc. Q2 2018 Earnings Transcript." *Seeking Alpha*, July 17, 2018.

Muller, Joann. "Exclusive: Inside New CEO Mary Barra's Urgent Mission to Fix GM." *Forbes*, May 28, 2014.

Benoit, David, and Allison Prang. "Carl Icahn to Launch New Board Fight With Xerox." *Wall Street Journal*, December 12, 2017.

"Paul Polman: In His Own Words." *Financial Times*, December 3, 2017.

Benzkofer, Marjorie. "The Authenticity Gap." FleishmanHillard, August, 18 2018. https://fleishmanhillard.com/2019/08/reputation-management/the-authenticity-gap.

Shrage, Michael. "Great CEOs See the Importance of Being Understood." *Harvard Business Review*, December 16, 2016.

Chapter 8

Eisen, Ben, and Emily Glazer. "Dimon's Remarks on Trump, Charlottesville Provoke Discussion Inside J.P. Morgan." *Wall Street Journal*, August 17, 2017

Eccles, Robert G., Scott C. Newquist, and Roland Schatz. "Reputation and Its Risks." *Harvard Business Review*, February 2007.

Scialpi, Davide. "Paul Polman's quotes about Success and Leadership." *Medium*, May 13, 2018. https://www.medium.com/@davidescialpi/paul-polmans-quotes-about-success-and-leadership-ceo-of-unilever-52af-f401a105.

Rutenberg, Jim. "For Disney's Iger, An Unlikely Political Turn." *New York Times*, October 8, 2017.

Blankfein, Lloyd. Interview by Jim Cramer. *Mad Money*. CNBC, June 19, 2017. https://www.cnbc.com/2017/06/19/cnbc-exclusive-cnbc-transcript-goldman-sachs-chairman-ceo-lloyd-blankfein-speaks-with-cnbcs-jim-cramer-on-mad-money-today.html.

Mathews, Anna Wilde. "Anthem's Boss Faces Tough Choices in Health-Care Debate." *Wall Street Journal*, June 13, 2017.

Bergman, Stanley M. "'Don't Leave People Behind,' Says CEO of the Year Stan Bergman." Speech, July, 20, 2017. *Chief Executive.* https://www.chiefexecutive.net/stan-bergman-ceoy-speech.

Edelman, Richard "Reimagining Our Profession Public Relations for a Complex World." Speech, institute for Public Relations annual Distinguished Lecture and Awards, November 10, 2011. https://www.instituteforpr.org/wp-content/uploads/Edelman-Lecture-November-10.pdf

"2019 Edelman Trust Barometer," January 20, 2019. https://www.edelman.com/trust-barometer

Browne, John with Robin Nuttall and Tommy Stadlen. *Connect: How Companies Succeed By Engaging Radically With Society.* London: W.H. Allen, 2015.

Dick's Sporting Goods. "United in Sport." Advertisement. *Chicago Tribune,* February 11, 2018.

Kasich, John with Daniel Paisner. *Two Paths: America Divided or United.* New York, NY: Thomas Dunne Books, 2017.

Panetta, Leon with Jim Newton. *Worthy Fights: A Memoir of Leadership in War and Peace.* New York, NY: Penguin Books, 2014.

Modzelewski, Jack. "Voters Didn't Like the Product That Politics Was Selling." *PRWeek,* November 10, 2016.

Baker, Gerard. "Davos 2017: Aristocrats Face the Pitchforks." *Wall Street Journal,* January 16, 2017.

Barrett, Steve. "Despite the Skeptics, Davos Is All Business." *PRWeek,* January 24, 2019.

Winfrey, Oprah. "Acceptance speech for the Cecil B. DeMille Lifetime Achievement Award." Golden Globes, January 6, 2018.

Final Thoughts

Noonan, Peggy. "How to Find a Good Leader." *Wall Street Journal,* November 1, 2018.

Modzelewski, Jack, and J.J. Carter. "How PR Pros Can Turn Smart CEOs Into Dynamic Communicators." *PR News,* March 7, 2016.

Index

ABC News, 39–40, 195
advocacy, xii, 8, 118, 152–153, 165, 189
Affordable Care Act (ACA), 17–18
Ahmadinejad, Mahmoud, 184
Ahrendts, Angela, 65
AIG, *see* American International Group
Airbnb, 65, 146
Alexa (Amazon), 92
Alibaba, 19, 65
Allstate Prosperity Report, 21
Amazon, 8, 27, 65, 101, 107, 142
American Airlines, 28, 123–124
American International Group (AIG), 69
American Society of News Editors, 107
American Turnaround (Whitacre), 136
Ameritech, 134
Anbang, 12
Anthem, 173–174
Apple, 65, 158, 159, 172–173
Argenti, Paul, 11–12
Armstrong, Lance, 49
Arthur Andersen, 36
Arthur W. Page Society, 123, 131
artificial intelligence (AI), 71, 91–92, 140
Associated Press, 68
AT&T, 119, 121, 133–135, 140, 150
Aung San Suu Kyi, 185–186
authentic communications, xii, 19, 20, 31, 99, 157, 194–197
Avon, 12

Backpage, 12
Baker, Gerard, 181–182
Bandurski, David, 103
Barclays LLC, 12
Barings Bank, 36
Barra, Mary, 36–37, 149
Barrett, Steve, 118, 133, 181
Baxter International, 23, 150
BCG, 159
Bear Stearns, 69
Bechtel, 122
Beck, Scott, 1, 9
Beijing Normal University, 183
BellSouth, 134
Bergman, Stanley, 174
Bezos, Jeff, 8, 27, 101
Big Short, The (Lewis), 45
Bingol, Selim, 119, 135
Black Lives Matter, 167
BlackRock, 22–23, 152–153, 167–168
black swan crisis, 44, 69
Blankfein, Lloyd, 173
BlessingWhite, 7
Bloomberg, Michael, 13
Bloomberg News, 4, 99–100
Bono, 13

Booz Allen Hamilton, 159
BP, 68, 97, 150, 175–176
Bradberry, Travis, 94–95
brand study, 135–136
Brando, Marlon, 89, 97
Branson, Richard, 101–102
Brown, Dan, 34
Browne, Sir John, 175–176
Buffett, Warren, 13
Burberry, 65, 159
Burke, James, 41, 57
Burnett, Leo, 90
Burry, Michael, 45
Bush, George H. W., 194–195
Bush, George W., 69
Business Roundtable, 169, 171

Cal-Nev Pipeline, 81–82
Caterpillar, 12, 150
CBS, 12, 75
Cecil B. DeMille Lifetime Achievement Award, 187
Centers for Disease Control (CDC), 56
CEO Today, 9
Cervone, Tony, 131
Chambers, John, 20
change for the better, 143, 155–156, 184
Charles Schwab, 19
CHG Healthcare, 1, 9
Chicago Club, 20
Chicago Cubs, 161–164
chief communications officers (CCOs), 9–10, 29, 116–127, 128–132, 137
chief executive officers (CEOs), xi, 2–3, 5–6, 9–12, 33–34, 41, 55, 78, 117–118, 122–124, 157
  chief credibility officer, 95, 113, 115
  corporate narrative, 101–102
  creating expectations, 21
  credibility, xiii, 12–13, 71, 111, 135, 177
  reward systems, 21
Chief Executive, 11, 28, 123, 174
China Cyberspace Administration, 23
China Media Project, 103
Chipotle, 12, 24–25
Christmas Story, A (Shepherd), 195
Chrysler Corporation, 5, 69, 147–148, 159
Churchill, Winston, xi, 7, 188
Cisco, 20
Citadel Capital, 20, 41–42
Citizens United for Baseball Sunshine (CUBS), 161–162
Clinton, Bill, 178
CNBC, 5, 98, 141, 150, 153, 172, 173
Coca-Cola, 102
communications technology, 104, 115, 127, 144, 154, 165
Connect (Browne), 175
ConocoPhillips, 97
Control Risks, 78–79
  "RiskMap", 79
Converse, 159
Cook, Fred, 81–82
Cook, Tim, 158, 172–173
Coolidge, Cavin, 170
Council on American-Islamic Relations, 164
Cramer, Jim, 141, 173
credibility, xiii, 12–13, 71, 95, 111, 122, 115, 128, 135, 177
crisis, 24–25, 33–43, 46–50, 55–59, 60–62, 63, 65, 68–85, 86–87, 98–99, 148–149
  categories, 43–46
  3-R apology, 50–53
  "Ten Commandments of Crisis Management", 59–60
C-SPAN, 195
culture, 2, 17–29, 30–31, 70–72, 75, 111
  microcultures, 22
  misalignment, 123–124
  values, 87, 93

Daley, Richard M., 73, 182
Dao, David, 38–39
Dartmouth University, 11
Deepwater Horizon, 97, 176
Defenders of Human Rights Center, 184
Dell Corporation, 74–75
Dell, Michael, 75
De Niro, Robert, 155
Delta Airlines, 159
Dick's Sporting Goods, 176–177
Diddy (Sean Combs), 47–48
Dimon, Jamie, 13, 167, 168–169, 170
disaster recovery, 50, 59–60, 120–121
Disney, Walt, 66
do Rego Barros, Paulino, Jr., 52–53

Donaldson, Sam, 195
Draghi, Mario, 173
Drucker, Peter, 19
Dudley, Robert, 97, 176
Duke Energy, 119
Dunne, Finley Peter, 110

Easterbrook, Steve, 141–143
Ebadi, Shirin, 184
Eberwein, Elise, 28–29, 123–124
Eccles, Robert, 169
Economic Club of Chicago, 22, 100, 169
Economist, 25, 103
Edelman, Richard, 175
Edelman Trust Barometer, 175
Egon Zehnder, xiii, 117
Elizabeth Arden, 102
Elliott Management, 80
Emanuel, Rahm, 149
Emerson, Ralph Waldo, 9
emotional intelligence, 94–95, 109–110
Enron, 36
Epstein, Theo, 161
Equifax, 12, 51–53
Expedia, 27

Facebook, 105–107, 118–119, 158
Fannie Mae, 69
FedEx, 93, 122
Feinberg, Kenneth, 37
Feinstein, Dianne, 173
Fiat, 159
Fields, Mark, 4–6
FIFA, 12
Fink, Laurence, 22–23, 152–153, 167–168
Firestone, 45–46
Fitzgerald, F. Scott, 26
FleishmanHillard, 17–19, 134–135, 157
  "The Authenticity Gap," 157
Flickr, 197
Forbes, 94, 101, 102, 149
Ford Motor Company, 3–6, 12, 45–46
Ford, Bill, 3
Ford, Henry, 3
Formula, The, 89, 97
Fortune, 29, 42, 110, 117
Fox News, 12, 68, 150
Freddie Mac, 69

GAAP reporting, 126
Galloway, Scott, 144
Gallup, 1, 2
Gates, Bill, 160
GATX, 82
General Electric, 7–8, 12, 29, 117
General Motors, 36–37, 69, 119, 131, 136, 149
Gerstner, Lou, 21
Get Covered Illinois, 17
Gillibrand, Kirsten, 188
Gladwell, Malcolm, xiv
Golden Globe Awards, 187
Goldman Sachs, 69, 173
Golin, 2, 81–82, 205
Golin-U.S.C. Annenberg Global Relevance Review, 2
Google, 107
Graham, John, 135
Greenpeace, 53–54
Greenspan, Alan, 45
Grenesko, Don, 162–164
Griffin, Ken, 20, 41–42
Grove, Andrew, 33

Hammerstein, Oscar, 196
Harris, Kamala, 173
Harris, Steve, 148
Harty, Harriet, 21
Harvard Business Review, 160, 169
Hathaway, Anne, 155
Hays, Andy, 162
Hemingway, Ernest, 12
Hennes & Mauritz, 47
Henry Schein, 174
Henson, James, 58–59
Herbette, Guillaume, 92
Hilton, 122
Huffington, Arianna, 26
Hurricane Katrina, 45

Iacocca, Lee, 147–148
Icahn, Carl, 80, 151–152
Iger, Robert, 171–172
Ignatius, David, 34
Instagram, 91, 139, 143, 158

Institute for Public Relations, 175
Intel, 12, 33
Intern, The, 154

James, LeBron, 47
Jarvis, Rebecca, 39–40
Jenkins, Holman W., Jr., 97, 169–170
Jewel Food Stores, 58–59
JPMorgan, 150, 167, 168–169

Kaiser Permanente, 127–128
Kalanick, Travis, 25–27, 51
Kasich, John, 177
Kasparov, Gary, 184–185
Kenny Construction Company, 73
Ketchum, 2
Khosrowshahi, Dara, 27, 51
Kimmel, Jimmy, 39
King Abdullah City for Atomic and Renewable Energy (KA-CARE), 95
King, Martin Luther, Jr., 199–200
Kline, Richard, 82
Knowlege@Wharton, 120
Kobe Steel, 12
Kodak, 152
Korn Ferry, 128–129, 155
KPMG, 150
Kraemer, Harry Janssen, Jr., 23
KRC Research, 98
Kumar, Abhinav, 124–125

Lafley, A.G., 150
Lagarde, Christine, 13
Lee, Robert E., 168
Lego, 159
Lehman Brothers, 42, 69
Lessons from the Top, 7
Lewis, Michael, 45
Lightfoot, Lori, 182
LinkedIn, 10
Liu Xiaobo, 183
Livestrong, 49
Long-Term Capital Management, 36
Lutz, Robert, 5–6

Ma, Jack, 19
Magna Carta, 100
Mahindra, Anand, 13
Mandela, Nelson, 174, 183, 184
Margaritis, Bill, 93, 95, 122
Marriot International, 23
Marvel, 159
McCarthy, Kevin, 173
McDonald, Bob, 150
McDonald's Corporation, 56, 141–143
McKinsey & Company, 27
media negotiations, 109–111
Medill School of Journalism, Media, Integrated Marketing Communications, 99, 103
Medvedev, Dmitry, 185
Merriam-Webster, 35
mission-driven communications, 10, 93
Modi, Narenda, 13
Mohammed bin Rashid Al Maktoum, 10
Mohammed bin Salman, 96
Monsanto, 150
Morgan Stanley, 146
MSLGroup, 92
Montgomery, Walter, 120
Mulally, Alan, 3–4, 6
Mulva, James, 97
Munoz, Oscar, 39–40
Musk, Elon, 5

Nabisco, 21
Nadella, Satya, 95, 160
NASA, 121
Netflix, 159
Newquist, Scott, 169
NewsCorp, 107
New York Times, The, 81, 110, 172
New Yorker, The, 75
NGOs, 8, 22, 59–60, 71, 79, 83, 119, 167, 175, 180–181, 189
Niccol, Brian, 25
Nike, 191
Nobel Prize, xi, 183, 184, 185, 186
Nocera, Joe, 4
non-PR problems, 46–48
Nooyi, Indra, 17
NORAD, 121
Nostradamus, 131

Obama, Barack, 47, 91
O'Donnell, Norah, 104
Olympus, 12
Omnicom Group, 146
On the Brink (Paulson), 69
Orwell, George, 145
Outliers (Gladwell), xiv

Pacific Bell, 134
paid media, 108–111
Panetta, Leon, 13, 177–178
Panetta Institute for Public Policy, 178
Parade, 104
Parker, Doug, 28, 123
Paulson, Henry "Hank", 69, 83, 173
Pearce, Terry, 7, 19
Peltz, Nelson, 150–151
People, 102
Pew Research Center 2017 American Trends Panel, 106
PepsiCo, 17
Perot, Ross, 100
personal brand, 8
Petrobras, 12
Polish National Alliance, 194
Polman, Paul, 13, 101, 153, 171
Pope Francis, 91
Priestley, Joseph, 89
privacy, 158
Procter & Gamble (P&G), 53–55, 150–151
Projeqt, 197
PRWeek, 49, 118, 123, 124, 125, 133, 179, 181
Publicis Groupe, 92
public policy, 152–153, 173–179, 189
public trust, 13, 46–47, 49, 52, 175–177, 192
Putin, Vladimir, 91, 185
PwC Global CEO Survey, 2

Reagan, Ronald, 4
Rehab, Ahmed, 164
relationships, 82–85, 127–128
  with communities, 11, 61
  with customers, 97
  with news media, 109–111
  with stakeholders, 71, 118, 125
reputation, 8–9, 12–13, 15, 24–25, 29, 40, 45–55, 63, 68, 76, 80–81, 95–96, 106, 151
  leadership responsibility, 89–90, 112, 116–118, 125, 127
  measurable asset, 9, 60
risk management, 50, 57, 60, 62, 63, 65–72, 77–80, 82–85, 86–87, 124, 148–149, 170
  risk identification, 70–72, 87, 192–193
  worst-case-scenario planning, 66
Robinson, Janet, 115
Robinson Lehrer & Montgomery, 120
Roddenberry, Gene, 8
Rodgers, Richard, 196
Rohingya, 186
Roosevelt, Eleanor, 169
Royal Ascot, 119
Rubenstein, David, 13, 99–101
Rubin, Robert, 173
Rutenberg, Jim, 172

Samson, Dave, 123, 125
Sandberg, Sheryl, 13
SBC Communications, 133–136
Schatz, Roland, 169
Schrager, Ian, 146
Schultz, Howard, 13, 142
Scion Capital, 45
Sears, 36
shareholder activism, 80, 152
Sheffer, Gary, 29, 117
Shepherd, Jean, 195
Singer, Mark, 75
Sloan, Timothy, 51
Smith, Frederick, 13, 93
Snapchat, 91
social media, 39, 47–48, 52, 61–62, 67, 79, 91, 102, 104–108, 117, 118–119, 121, 126, 144, 158, 182–183, 189
social responsibility, 171, 175
Sondheim, Stephen, 196
Sonnenfeld, Jeffrey, 11
Sony, 74–75
Sotheby's, 100
Southern Pacific, 81
Stack, Edward, 177

stakeholders, 1, 66, 125–126, 136, 143, 151, 170, 192
  stakeholder engagement, xii, 9, 10, 50, 61, 71, 98, 118–119, 123
Stanford Graduate School of Business, 69
Starbucks, 142
Starmann, Dick, 56
Stengel, Casey, 199
Stern School of Business, 13
Stevenson, Adlai, II, 143
storyteller in chief, xi, 101, 102–105
storytelling, 90–92, 99–102, 105–108, 112–113, 197
Stringer, Howard, 75
success syndrome, 143
Sun Also Rises, The (Hemingway), 12
Swedish, Joseph, 173–174
Systrom, Kevin, 139, 143

Taco Bell, 25
Takeda, 12
Target, 12
Tata Consultancy Services, 124
Taylor, David, 150–151
Tesla, 5–6
The New York Times Company, 115
The Walt Disney Company, 171
The White House, 95, 149, 172, 178, 195
Tillerson, Rex, 96–97
Tokyo Electric Power, 12
Tour de France, 49
Troubled Asset Relief Program (TARP), 37
Trump, Donald, 91, 168, 170, 172, 178–179
Tuck School of Business, 11
Tutu, Desmond, 184
Twain, Mark, 191, 192
Twitter, 39, 91, 118, 151, 158, 182, 187
Two Paths (Kasich), 177
Tylenol crisis, 41, 57
Tyson, Bernard, 13
Tyson Foods, 12

Uber, 12, 25–27, 51, 142, 146
Unilever, 101, 153, 171
United Airlines, 38–39
United Nations, 186
Univision, 164
U.S. Airways, 28
U.S. Chamber of Commerce, 171
U.S. Department of Commerce, 122
U.S. Federal Reserve, 45
U.S. Securities and Exchange Commission, 192
U.S. Treasury Department, 69, 173

Viacom, 107
Vimeo, 197
Virgin Group, 101–102
Volcker, Paul, 13
Volkswagen, 12, 23–24

Walesa, Lech, 184
Wall Street Journal, The, 6, 12, 21, 26, 38, 52, 76, 97, 132, 133, 143, 146, 151–152, 168–170, 173, 181, 192
Walmart, 93–94
Walton, Sam, 93–94
Wang Jianlin, 13
Washington, Harold, 163, 182
Washington Post, The, 183
Wasserman, Lew, 7
Weber Shandwick
  2017 Report from the Buy Side, 98
Weinstein, Harvey, 48
Weinstein Company, 12
Welch, Jack, 7–8, 98, 199–200
Wells Fargo, 12, 50–51
Whitacre, Edward, Jr., 133–136
Whitman, Meg, 13
Winfrey, Oprah, 13, 49, 91, 187
Witherspoon, Reese, 102
Woebcken, Hinrich, 24
World Economic Forum, 33–34, 44, 122, 153, 171, 179–182, 199
Worthy Fights: A Memoir of Leadership in War and Peace (Panetta), 178
Wren, John, 146
Wynn Resorts, 12

Xerox, 151–152
Xi Jinping, 103

Yale School of Management, 11
YouTube, 102, 195, 197

Zuckerberg, Mark, 100, 105

About the Author

Jack Modzelewski is founder and chief executive of JackKnifePR, a business communications consulting firm in Chicago. His extensive career in public relations, marketing, communications, and executive management included roles with global agencies. Most notably, he was president of FleishmanHillard, where he worked for more than twenty-six years in executive and international positions, including five years as president of Europe and Africa and nearly five as president of the Americas.

Modzelewski has more than thirty-five years of experience with corporate and brand communications programs for a wide spectrum of big clients in the telecommunications, automotive, food service, technology, energy, financial, healthcare, and professional sports industries. He has worked with companies such as McDonald's, AT&T, General Motors, Chase Bank, Baxter, Tribune, Monsanto, and Procter & Gamble. He also advised associations such as the Consumer Electronics Association and not-for-profits such as St. Jude Children's Research Hospital.

He has considerable firsthand experience in corporate and financial communications, mergers, and organizational restructurings, issues management, and all means of strategic stakeholder outreach. He has assisted clients in twenty-five major crises, both domestic and international. One of Modzelewski's past clients called him the "counsellor's counsellor."

He has given speeches and written articles on subjects spanning leadership, international business, marketing and social media, and risk and crisis management. He's attended five World Economic Forum (WEF) conferences in Davos and WEF meetings on five continents. He has been listed on *PRWeek*'s Global Power List and in 2015 was inducted in the Medill Hall of Achievement at Northwestern University. He is currently chairman of the board of the Better Government Association in Illinois and also sits on the Medill board. Prior to his career in public relations and communications, he was a multimedia, award-winning journalist.